AMERICAN POETS PROJECT

The American Poets Project is published

with a gift in memory of
JAMES MERRILL

and support from the
SIDNEY J. WEINBERG, JR. FOUNDATION

American Wits

an anthology of light verse

john hollander editor

AMERICAN POETS PROJECT

THE LIBRARY OF AMERICA

Some of the material in this volume is reprinted with permission of the holders of copyright and publication rights. Acknowledgments are on pages 175–80.

The paper used in this publication meets the minimum requirements of the American National Standard for Information Sciences—Permanence of Paper for Printed Library materials, ANSI Z39.48—1984.

Design by Chip Kidd and Mark Melnick.

Library of Congress Cataloging in Publication Data:
American wits: an anthology of light verse / John Hollander, editor.
      p. cm. — (American poets project)
   Includes bibliographical references and index.
   ISBN 1–931082–49–9 (alk. paper)
      1. Humorous poetry, American. 2. American poetry. I. Hollander, John.
      II. Series.
   PS595.H8A44 2003
   811'.0708 — dc21
   2003046636

   10 9 8 7 6 5 4 3 2 1

CONTENTS

INTRODUCTION

The American wits collected here were for the most part not poets in the fullest (or full-time) sense of the word. Many were primarily journalists, playwrights, or screenwriters (some were all those things). They were, however, immensely skillful writers of verse, and the ways in which they set about being funny in verse rather than in prose shaped their whole literary mode. Their work is marked by dexterity and sharpness and a manifest pleasure in what they were doing.

They lived and worked at a fortunate moment in the history of modern literacy: they could count on the kind of gently but firmly educated middlebrow audience that still constituted a "popular" one. Their work defined a particular sort of 20th-century American urbanity, tougher and a bit grittier than in earlier eras. (While the volume begins with Ambrose Bierce in the late 19th century and concludes with some work from recent decades, the kind of verse it focuses on enjoyed its heyday from about 1920 through the mid-century.) Much of the material in this volume from before World War II represents the sort of poetry that regularly appeared in those days in newspaper columns, such as Franklin P. Adams' celebrated *The Conning Tower*. These writers' skeptical attitudes toward love, sex, money, authority, and officially proclaimed sources of wisdom generally partake of the wisecracking that began to dominate so much American comic writing, song, and film after World War I. At the same time, their ambivalent relationship to "serious" poetry reflects a tradition going back to the 18th century or even earlier.

For the most part they were not literati scornful of the middlebrow, but very clever high-middlebrows themselves, who nonetheless scorned the vulgarities of pretentiousness and nascent consumerism. These were not modernist poets. But their turn away from the benign geniality of most of the comic verse of the preceding era parallels the reaction of high modernist poetry against the sentimental, expository, and narrative elements of much Victorian poetry. The sharpest of the light verse gathered here seems somehow in sympathy with that modernist sensibility, even though it may outwardly and playfully mock it.

The high poetic pretensions of literary modernism were marked by impersonality, irony, and a positive hostility to sentimentality. The American wits celebrated here developed an analogous mode of ironic self-criticism that was nonetheless sometimes not far removed from a sentimentality of its own. Consider Edna St. Vincent Millay's well-known "First Fig":

> My candle burns at both ends;
>   It will not last the night;
> But ah, my foes, and oh, my friends—
>   It gives a lovely light!

When this was first published, its outright confession would have been somewhat shocking: "A *young woman* mustn't talk like Byron!" It is now for us quite sentimental, although redeemed by the pointed contrast between the meanings of "ah" and "oh" in the third line.

Dorothy Parker's "News Item"—"Men seldom make passes / At girls who wear glasses"—is by contrast both light verse and unequivocally epigrammatic in the neo-classic mode of 18th-century poets like Pope and Prior. For them, epigram was a legitimate poetic genre going back to the Greek Anthology and the Latin poets, a genre that in the hands of poets from Martial to Ben Jonson was the primary mode of written jokes before the modern form of the short oral fiction with punch-line. By the early 19th century, the genre had become marginalized, al-though we still have a continuing tradition of Martialian or Alexandrian epigram, exemplified by the American poet J. V. Cunningham's "Arms and the man I sing, and sing with joy, / Who was last year all elbows and a boy," or his "Naked I came, naked I leave the scene / And naked was my pastime in between." But I should not call these light verse at all, but rather the brilliant exercise of an art by a worthy poetic heir of Ben Jonson.

The speaker's voice in the poems collected here is edu-cated, often knowledgeable, at times somewhat snobbishly anti-intellectual; but its debunking, mildly antithetical stance shares something with the sensibility of high mod-ernism. It is always the voice of a speaker who despises—implicitly or explicitly—the kinds of vulgarity in public rhetoric (in advertising, political discourse, and all the un-relenting engines of sentimentality) that modernism so de-tested. For the geniality of earlier light verse, the writers in this volume substituted an exuberant irreverence.

"Light verse" need not be pointedly funny, or even (as it tends to be) mildly amusing. Here it should be remembered that, while popular usage suggests that "serious" and "funny" are mutually exclusive opposites, what is funny can also be very serious. This happens most often by design—by the design of wit. Likewise, what is solemn can be deeply frivolous, though usually inadvertently—and here, again, it will be some kind of wit that points out this shortcoming.

Some of the comic verse in these pages may raise questions of what it is that a particular comic poem is being serious *about*. Verse of this kind frequently mocks, chides, teases, or undermines a purported topic or rhetorical stance or convention; it can even joke about its own attitudes of indignation or amusement or attachment or detachment. But the best such verse seems somehow, no matter what its momentary concerns, to make light of high poetic seriousness itself. It borrows high literary art's most sacred vestments as costuming for its own entertainments and games.

Among those whose work is included in this volume are major poets such as T. S. Eliot, Robert Frost, Edwin Arlington Robinson, Ezra Pound, Edna St. Vincent Millay, John Crowe Ransom, W. H. Auden, James Merrill, and Anthony Hecht. Such poets, despite their very different voices, often sound more like one another when writing light verse than in their principal work. This may be because, throughout the 20th century, light verse has been acknowledged as a mode of writing all its own. The Muse of these wits calls for a kind of *finish* scorned by the spirit of modern art. It was finish that modernist aesthetics started avoiding in painting and later in the genres and diction of poetry, so that there was always something naughty about "serious" poets writing light verse in the 20th century.

Perhaps the goal sought by writers of light verse might be thought of as a sublimity of surface. The one matter about which comic poems often seem unavowedly serious is the skill displayed in their own construction. Dorothy Parker makes the point explicitly in the last lines of "Fighting Words":

> Say I'm neither brave nor young,
>   Say I woo and coddle care,
> Say the devil touched my tongue,—
>   Still you have my heart to wear.
>
> But say my verses do not scan,
>   And I get me another man!

Parker's readers at the time (the poem was first collected in 1926) and over a couple of subsequent generations might have heard in her rhetorical pattern an echo of the Romantic poet Leigh Hunt's anthology piece, "Jenny Kiss'd Me": "Say I'm weary, say I'm sad, / Say that health and wealth have miss'd me, / Say I'm growing old, but add, / Jenny kiss'd me." More important, they would have understood what it meant for verses to scan at all, and particularly why metrical perfection, and even ingenuity, were necessary in order for comic verse to be acutely witty.

Perhaps this is why, as some of the best critics of light verse like Louis Kronenberger and William Harmon have pointed out, there is more great poetry than good light verse. (One tries to forget how much more very bad poetry there is than either of these.) We are today in a literary age of what jazz musicians used to call a tin ear; there is less light verse written, and probably less capacity to appreciate it, than ever before. Many attempts result in appallingly inept doggerel. When light verse by journalists appears in print today, there are few readers left who can judge its proficiency. Nowadays, most bad poetry is in free verse (that being the default mode, as inept rhyming used to be before World War II), and few readers and writers can hear the difference between incompetent and well-handled *vers libre*, or judge when the ineptitude is intended deliberately as something to laugh about.

The writers gathered here came to literate maturity at a time when the ability to read and write accentual-syllabic verse was part of what it meant to be literate. Up through World War II, a good many newspaper journalists throughout the country could from time to time scribble unembarrassing occasional verses; it was not assumed that to write in rhyme automatically made one a poet. There was something like a culture of verse, and all sorts of non-poets could and did produce excellent writing in rhyme.

One need have no pretensions to poetic imagination in order to write effective and amusing light verse. One does, on the other hand, need expert control, not only of meter and rhythm, but of diction, tone, and the mastery of scale and timing that in the musical theater was called "build." Light verse provides a perfect occasion for the display of such control. Byron's comic narrative *Beppo* might be cited as the first major example in English of light verse that was neither literary epigram nor song-text. Its amused deployment of the same complex poly-syllabic rhyming that he later used throughout *Don Juan* became basic material for later light verse. From W. S. Gilbert's rhyming, in *Iolanthe*, of "amorous dove / type of Ovidius Naso" with "Although I dare not say so," to Lorenz Hart's Morgan Le Fay (in the musical *A Connecti-cut Yankee*) listing the sequence of husbands she'd killed off with varied m.o.'s:

Sir Paul was frail. He looked a wreck to me
At night he was a horse's neck to me*
So I performed an appendectomy
To keep my love alive

Comic verse displayed additional virtuosity, particularly in the first half of the 20th century, by using French lyric forms imported by belle-lettristic minor British verse starting in the 1870s. Rondeaux and ballades were common, with refrains that often made use of playful puns. In cases like these, as more generally in pointed light verse, the verse form seems, so to speak, exoskeletal: foregrounded, not merely to display skill, but to express the sheer pleasure taken in employing it. The writer is permitted to show off, never with a swagger, but with a little laugh of delight.

Light verse can also involve surprise, playing games with expectations about formal or rhetorical conventions which are confirmed and at the same time overturned. But the games are never played for the imaginative stakes that we feel ride on high poetic seriousness; the goal is rather to allow the attentive reader to share the delight that the writer took in what he or she was doing. Robert Frost wrote of remembering with pleasure how he and

*A "horse's neck" was the name of a glass of ginger ale (and so designated on menus) in the 1930s and 40s, a device for allowing a consumer of same not to offend the serious drinkers at the table by his or her abstention. But the trope here, of a dysfunctional sexual companion, remains clear in any case. (The resonant and brilliant lines of witty—rather than sentimental—popular standard song lyrics, particularly the sharpest ones of Cole Porter, Lorenz Hart, Ira Gershwin, Johnny Mercer, Frank Loesser, Betty Comden and Adolph Green, and Stephen Sondheim, which might well have been included here, will be the subject of a future volume in this series.)

Ezra Pound (in London in 1915) laughed over the last line in a stanza of Edwin Arlington Robinson's "Miniver Cheevy"—

> Miniver scorned the gold he sought,
>   But sore annoyed was he without it;
> Miniver thought, and thought, and thought,
>   And thought about it.

—and the brilliance of the fourth "thought." (Frost said that it "made the intolerable touch of poetry.") The line is a particularly brilliant instance of the "build" mentioned above. Although the progression through the first three "thoughts" seems to suggest gradual deepening, it is only with the supererogatory final one that we are reminded that Miniver's "thought" is the soused rambling of a drunk. We are also reminded that the short fourth line in stanzas like the one used throughout the poem tends to have the tone of an afterthought, or qualifying remark; this stanza ratifies that implication with near sublimity.

The writers in this book were schooled in the whole tradition of British light verse in the 19th century, exemplified by Byron, Winthrop Mackworth Praed, Charles Stuart Calverley, Arthur Hugh Clough, Edward Lear, W. S. Gilbert, and Lewis Carroll, many of whose devices, strategies, and rhetorical stances helped frame the work not only of the "wits" represented here, but of some of their American precursors as well. Starting after World War I, however, there have been some particular American innovations in the forms of light verse.

Foremost among these is the stylistic mode of Ogden Nash. His unprecedented originality lay in taking the metrical default mode of bad doggerel—verse that rhymes but doesn't scan—and making of it a brilliantly devised system. He controls with an exquisite ear the variation in line length, adjusting the postponement of a rhyming word, or conversely, in a very short line, its presentation. His poems are as highly crafted and as pointed in their various sorts of joking as the most meticulous Victorian or modern *vers de société*.

"Light" free verse might seem a contradictory notion. Some early modernists were almost religiously devoted to free verse as an emblem of poetic purity, and they implicitly regarded the most solemn modes of their immediate precursors as unwittingly but necessarily light. But leaving aside the free-verse epigrams of D. H. Lawrence (in *Pansies*, for example), we might consider as almost unique the *vers libre* of the newspaper writer Don Marquis' Archy.

The delightful body of verse composed by this literary cockroach—who in a previous incarnation was, as he tells us, "a vers libre bard"—was supposed to have been written with tremendous physical effort as Archy jumped from key to key of the typewriter of his "boss," Marquis himself. Lower-case type was Archy's format, as it was of early Imagist poetry and of E. E. Cummings—but in Archy's case it was not by choice but because he was unable simultaneously to hold down a shift key and jump. Archy wrote of himself and of the splendid cat Mehitabel, a world-weary sophisticate who prowled the realms of tough urban life and who frequently composed elegantly crafted ballades to accompany Archy's free verse.

Kenneth Fearing, a pointedly and passionately radical poet of the 1930s and 40s, wrote all his work in free verse; some of it must count as satirical poetry, but, along with that of Cummings, a good deal of his work may represent a borderline case. Because I admire it and because it has been largely inaccessible for some decades, I include a sampling of Fearing's polemically charged wit.

Among other innovative forms there is the double dactyl. Analogous to the limerick and the very British clerihew, it has a purely American origin, being the invention of a major poet, Anthony Hecht, and a professor of classics, the late Paul Pascal. Like the limerick, it has a strict metrical form (two stanzas with three lines of two dactyls each and a short fourth line with one dactyl and a single stressed syllable, these two short lines rhyming). Like the clerihew, it emerges from the enunciation of a proper name—in this case, though, the name must occupy the second double-dactylic line, and the second stanza must contain one line occupied by a singled double-dactylic word. Here is Pascal's glowing exemplar (and consider the hilariously enjambed penultimate line):

> Patty-cake, patty-cake
> Marcus Antonius
> What do you think of the
> African queen?
>
> Gubernatorial
> Duties require my
> Presence in Egypt. Ya
> Know what I mean?

Examples of the form by Anthony Hecht, as well as by James Merrill and George Starbuck, will be found in this volume. The editor has excluded his own under the implicit pressure of E. E. Cummings' lines (of indubitable light verse):

> mr u will not be missed
> who as an anthologist
> sold the many on the few
> not excluding mr u

A fourth 20th-century American invention is that of William Cole, in his little volume called *Uncoupled Couplets*. In each of these, a celebrated line of English verse (most often in tetrameter or pentameter) will be rhymed with a new one, always debunking or otherwise deconstructive. The first line of Robert Herrick's "Upon Julia's Clothes" must have seemed to Cole like a curve ball that didn't break but hung, so that it was one's moral duty to hit it out of the ball park. And thus:

> Whenas in silks my Julia goes,
> *The outline of her girdle shows.*

Ultimately, all these writers were having serious fun with what they were doing. They took delight not only in what they had to say but in their precise manner of saying it. Under all the playfulness there is irreverence and a certain amount of satiric indignation, more civil than savage: but what makes it mean something is the exercise of craft, and the unique pleasure that poets and readers alike can take in that craft.

John Hollander
2003

FROM **The Devil's Dictionary**

Corporal

Fiercely the battle raged and, sad to tell,
Our corporal heroically fell!
Fame from her height looked down upon the brawl
And said: "He hadn't very far to fall."

Elegy

The cur foretells the knell of parting day;
  The loafing herd winds slowly o'er the lea;
The wise man homeward plods; I only stay
  To fiddle-faddle in a minor key.

Two Men

There be two men of all mankind
    That I should like to know about;
But search and question where I will,
    I cannot ever find them out.

Melchizedek he praised the Lord,
    And gave some wine to Abraham;
But who can tell what else he did
    Must be more learned than I am.

Ucalegon he lost his house
    When Agamemnon came to Troy;
But who can tell me who he was—
    I'll pray the gods to give him joy.

There be two men of all mankind
    That I'm forever thinking on:
They chase me everywhere I go,—
    Melchizedek, Ucalegon.

A Mighty Runner

(Nicarchus)

The day when Charmus ran with five
In Arcady, as I'm alive,
He came in seventh.—"Five and one
Make seven, you say? It can't be done."—
Well, if you think it needs a note,
A friend in a fur overcoat
Ran with him, crying all the while,
"You'll beat 'em, Charmus, by a mile!"
And so he came in seventh.
Therefore, good Zoilus, you see
The thing is plain as plain can be;
And with four more for company,
He would have been eleventh.

Miniver Cheevy

Miniver Cheevy, child of scorn,
    Grew lean while he assailed the seasons;
He wept that he was ever born,
    And he had reasons.

Miniver loved the days of old
    When swords were bright and steeds were prancing;
The vision of a warrior bold
    Would set him dancing.

Miniver sighed for what was not,
  And dreamed, and rested from his labors;
He dreamed of Thebes and Camelot,
  And Priam's neighbors.

Miniver mourned the ripe renown
  That made so many a name so fragrant;
He mourned Romance, now on the town,
  And Art, a vagrant.

Miniver loved the Medici,
  Albeit he had never seen one;
He would have sinned incessantly
  Could he have been one.

Miniver cursed the commonplace
  And eyed a khaki suit with loathing;
He missed the mediæval grace
  Of iron clothing.

Miniver scorned the gold he sought,
  But sore annoyed was he without it;
Miniver thought, and thought, and thought,
  And thought about it.

Miniver Cheevy, born too late,
  Scratched his head and kept on thinking;
Miniver coughed, and called it fate,
  And kept on drinking.

CAROLYN WELLS | 1869–1942

Famous Baths and Bathers

The baths of Caracalla
Beat those in Walla Walla;
Their emblems and omens
Appealed to the Romans.

The baths of Diocletian
Were filled to repletion
With aediles and eunuchs
In togas and tunics.

Susanna, young fool,
Bathed in the pool;
The elders in the shrubbery
Kicked up a bobbery.

Diogenes, old chap,
Just turned on a tap;
(No, that couldn't be,
For he lived B.C.)

Brave Sir Launcelot
Liked the water hot;
While the old Ettrick shephe'd
Preferred his quite tepid.

Marat, we know,
Used a bathtub, and so
Was put out of the way
By Charlotte Corday.

All of the Pitts
Always used Sitz;
The family tradition
Decreed this position.

But E. Humperdinck
Washed at the sink;
He said, "It saves time
And it takes off the grime."

Elegy

The jackals prowl, the serpents hiss
In what was once Persepolis.
Proud Babylon is but a trace
Upon the desert's dusty face.
The topless towers of Ilium
Are ashes. Judah's harp is dumb.
The fleets of Nineveh and Tyre
Are down with Davy Jones, Esquire,
And all the oligarchies, kings,
And potentates that ruled these things
Are gone! But cheer up; don't be sad;
Think what a lovely time they had!

FROM **The Lyric Baedeker**

Philadelphia

I can lyricize ornately
Of the city that sedately
Stands upon the western bank of Delaware,
For I know a Lloyd, a Norris
And a Rittenhouse and Morris,
And I'm quite at home on Independence Square.

In the reign of Charles the Second,
Where the leafy forest beckoned
It was founded by a certain William Penn,
Whom the people speak quite well of;
And you also hear them tell of
Mr. Franklin, known familiarly as "Ben."

There are many colored voters,
And a reckless mob of motors,
And the streets are Market, Chestnut, Spruce, and Pine.
The descendants of the Quakers
Buy their pins at Wanamaker's,
And the Stratford is the proper place to dine.

When you pass the outer bound'ries
Of the textile mills and foundries,
Fairmount Park will yield contentment to the soul.
All the suburbs are alluring;
And their roads are fine for touring,
Though at every other mile you pay a toll.

Where the trees in April quicken
On the lovely Wissahickon,
Or in winter where the Schuylkill, full of slush,
Cuts the city through the middle,
One may even see a Biddle,
A Cadwallader, a Shippen, or a Rush!

You should tarry there and grapple
With the mysteries of "scrapple"—
A conglomerate of flour, herbs, and pork.
Philadelphia, not to quiz it,
Is a pleasant place—to *visit*;
Which is what the natives say about New York.

Seattle

Her earliest settlers, in brief,
   Arrived with their guns and their cattle,
And took from an Indian chief
   The site and the name of Seattle.

And now, with unanimous voice,
   Their progeny, brave and prolific,
Proclaim that the town of their choice
   Is Queen of the Azure Pacific!

Her thoroughfares bustle and hum;
   (Her neighboring ranges are glacial);
They boast that she hasn't a slum;
   Her dwellings are simply palatial.

Her lakes, newly joined to the Sound,
   Are rated as chief of her glories;
Her buildings are widely renowned—
   The tallest has forty-two stories!

Her death-rate's as low as can be;
  Her climate is bracing, yet balmy;
And every one tells you to see
  Her thundering Falls of Snoqualmie.

Her forested parkways invite
  The stranger with piney aroma;
Her citizens all are polite—
  Except when you flatter Tacoma.

Her maidens are none of them plain,
  You'll nowhere find men who are brainier;
And if she has plenty of rain,
  Her favorite mountain is Rainier.

Everything In Its Place

The skeleton is hiding in the closet as it should,
The needle's in the haystack and the trees are in the wood,
The fly is in the ointment and the froth is on the beer,
The bee is in the bonnet and the flea is in the ear.

The meat is in the coconut, the cat is in the bag,
The dog is in the manger and the goat is on the crag,
The worm is in the apple and the clam is on the shore,
The birds are in the bushes and the wolf is at the door.

On the Vanity of Earthly Greatness

The tusks that clashed in mighty brawls
Of mastodons, are billiard balls.

The sword of Charlemagne the Just
Is ferric oxide, known as rust.

The grizzly bear whose potent hug
Was feared by all, is now a rug.

Great Caesar's dead and on the shelf,
And I don't feel so well myself!

The Embarrassing Episode of Little Miss Muffet

Little Miss Muffet discovered a tuffet,
    (Which never occurred to the rest of us)
And, as 'twas a June day, and just about noonday
    She wanted to eat—like the best of us:
Her diet was whey, and I hasten to say
    It is wholesome and people grow fat on it.
The spot being lonely, the lady not only
    Discovered the tuffet, but sat on it.

A rivulet gabbled beside her and babbled,
    As rivulets always are thought to do,
And dragon-flies sported around and cavorted,
    As poets say dragon-flies ought to do;
When, glancing aside for a moment, she spied
    A horrible sight that brought fear to her,
A hideous spider was sitting beside her
    And most unavoidably near to her!

Albeit unsightly, this creature politely
    Said: "Madam, I earnestly vow to you,
I'm penitent that I did not bring my hat. I
    Should otherwise certainly bow to you."
Though anxious to please, he was so ill at ease
    That he lost all his sense of propriety,

And grew so inept that he clumsily stept
    In her plate—which is barred in Society.

This curious error completed her terror;
    She shuddered, and growing much paler, not
Only left tuffet, but dealt him a buffet
    Which doubled him up in a sailor-knot.
It should be explained that at this he was pained:
    He cried: "I have vexed you, no doubt of it!
Your fist's like a truncheon." "You're still in my luncheon,"
    Was all that she answered. "Get out of it!"

And THE MORAL is this: Be it madam or miss
    To whom you have something to say,
You are only absurd when you get in the curd
    But you're rude when you get in the whey.

The Harmonious Heedlessness of Little Boy Blue

Composing scales beside the rails
    That flanked a field of corn,
A farmer's boy with vicious joy
    Performed upon a horn:
The vagrant airs, the fragrant airs
    Around that field that strayed,
Took flight before the flagrant airs
    That noisome urchin played.

He played with care "The Maiden's Prayer;"
  He played "God Save the Queen,"
"Die Wacht am Rhein," and "Auld Lang Syne,"
  And "Wearing of the Green:"
With futile toots, and brutal toots,
  And shrill chromatic scales,
And utterly inutile toots,
  And agonizing wails.

The while he played, around him strayed,
  And calmly chewed the cud,
Some thirty-nine assorted kine,
  All ankle-deep in mud:
They stamped about and tramped about
  That mud, till all the troupe
Made noises, as they ramped about,
  Like school-boys eating soup.

Till, growing bored, with one accord
  They broke the fence forlorn:
The field was doomed. The cows consumed
  Two-thirds of all the corn,
And viciously, maliciously,
  Went prancing o'er the loam.
That landscape expeditiously
  Resembled harvest-home.

"Most idle ass of all your class,"
  The farmer said with scorn:
"Just see my son, what you have done!
  The cows are in the corn!"

"Oh drat," he said, "the brat!" he said.
    The cowherd seemed to rouse.
"My friend, it's worse than that," he said.
    "The corn is in the cows."

THE MORAL lies before our eyes.
    When tending kine and corn,
Don't spend your noons in tooting tunes
    Upon a blatant horn:
Or scaling, and assailing, and
    With energy immense,
Your cows will take a railing, and
    The farmer take offense.

The Wrights' Biplane

This biplane is the shape of human flight.
Its name might better be First Motor Kite.
Its makers' name—Time cannot get that wrong,
For it was writ in heaven doubly Wright.

In Divés' Dive

It is late at night and still I am losing,
But still I am steady and unaccusing.

As long as the Declaration guards
My right to be equal in number of cards,

It is nothing to me who runs the Dive.
Let's have a look at another five.

In a Poem

The sentencing goes blithely on its way,
And takes the playfully objected rhyme
As surely as it keeps the stroke and time
In having its undeviable say.

the song of mehitabel

this is the song of mehitabel
of mehitabel the alley cat
as i wrote you before boss
mehitabel is a believer
in the pythagorean
theory of the transmigration
of the soul and she claims
that formerly her spirit
was incarnated in the body
of cleopatra
that was a long time ago
and one must not be
surprised if mehitabel
has forgotten some of her
more regal manners

i have had my ups and downs
but wotthehell wotthehell
yesterday sceptres and crowns
fried oysters and velvet gowns
and today i herd with bums
but wotthehell wotthehell

i wake the world from sleep
as i caper and sing and leap
when i sing my wild free tune
wotthehell wotthehell
under the blear eyed moon
i am pelted with cast off shoon
but wotthehell wotthehell

do you think that i would change
my present freedom to range
for a castle or moated grange
wotthehell wotthehell
cage me and i d go frantic
my life is so romantic
capricious and corybantic
and i m toujours gai toujours gai

i know that i am bound
for a journey down the sound
in the midst of a refuse mound
but wotthehell wotthehell
oh i should worry and fret
death and i will coquette
there s a dance in the old dame yet
toujours gai toujours gai

i once was an innocent kit
wotthehell wotthehell

with a ribbon my neck to fit
and bells tied onto it
o wotthehell wotthehell
but a maltese cat came by
with a come hither look in his eye
and a song that soared to the sky
and wotthehell wotthehell
and i followed adown the street
the pad of his rhythmical feet
o permit me again to repeat
wotthehell wotthehell

my youth i shall never forget
but there s nothing i really regret
wotthehell wotthehell
there s a dance in the old dame yet
toujours gai toujours gai

the things that i had not ought to
i do because i ve gotto
wotthehell wotthehell
and i end with my favorite motto
toujours gai toujours gai

boss sometimes i think
that our friend mehitabel
is a trifle too gay

      archy

archy at the zoo

the centipede adown the street
goes braggartly with scores of feet
a gaudy insect but not neat

the octopus s secret wish
is not to be a formal fish
he dreams that some time he may grow
another set of legs or so
and be a broadway music show

oh do not always take a chance
upon an open countenance
the hippopotamus s smile
conceals a nature full of guile

human wandering through the zoo
what do your cousins think of you

i worry not of what the sphinx
thinks or maybe thinks she thinks

i have observed a setting hen
arise from that same attitude
and cackle forth to chicks and men
some quite superfluous platitude

serious camel sad giraffe
are you afraid that if you laugh
those graceful necks will break in half

a lack of any mental outlet
dictates the young cetacean s spoutlet
he frequent blows like me and you
because there s nothing else to do

when one sees in the austral dawn
a wistful penguin perched upon
a bald man s bleak and desert dome
one knows tis yearning for its home

the quite irrational ichneumon
is such a fool it s almost human

despite the sleek shark s far flung grin
and his pretty dorsal fin
his heart is hard and black within
even within a dentist s chair
he still preserves a sinister air
a prudent dentist always fills
himself with gas before he drills

                              archy

FROM **mehitabel's extensive past**

i had some romantic
lives and some elegant times i
have seen better days archy but
whats the use of kicking kid its
all in the game like a gentleman
friend of mine used to say
toujours gai kid toujours gai he
was an elegant cat he used
to be a poet himself and he made up
some elegant poetry about me and him

lets hear it i said and
mehitabel recited

persian pussy from over the sea
demure and lazy and smug and fat
none of your ribbons and bells for me
ours is the zest of the alley cat
over the roofs from flat to flat
we prance with capers corybantic
what though a boot should break a slat
mehitabel us for the life romantic

we would rather be rowdy and gaunt and free
and dine on a diet of roach and rat

roach i said what do you
mean roach interrupting mehitabel
yes roach she said thats the
way my boy friend made it up
i climbed in amongst the typewriter
keys for she had an excited
look in her eyes go on mehitabel i
said feeling safer and she
resumed her elocution

we would rather be rowdy and gaunt and free
and dine on a diet of roach and rat
than slaves to a tame society
ours is the zest of the alley cat
fish heads freedom a frozen sprat
dug from the gutter with digits frantic
is better than bores and a fireside mat
mehitabel us for the life romantic

when the pendant moon in the leafless tree
clings and sways like a golden bat
i sing its light and my love for thee
ours is the zest of the alley cat
missiles around us fall rat a tat tat
but our shadows leap in a ribald antic
as over the fences the world cries scat
mehitabel us for the life romantic

persian princess i dont care that
for your pedigree traced by scribes pedantic
ours is the zest of the alley cat
mehitabel us for the life romantic

aint that high brow stuff
archy i always remembered it
but he was an elegant gent
even if he was a highbrow and a
regular bohemian archy him and
me went aboard a canal boat
one day and he got his head into
a pitcher of cream and couldn t get
it out and fell overboard
he come up once before he
drowned toujours gai kid he
gurgled and then sank for ever that
was always his words archy toujours
gai kid toujours gai i
have known some swell gents
in my time dearie

ballade of the under side

by archy
the roach that scurries
skips and runs
may read far more than those
that fly
i know what family skeletons

within your closets
swing and dry
not that i ever
play the spy
but as in corners
dim i bide
i can t dodge knowledge
though i try
i see things from
the under side

the lordly ones the
haughty ones
with supercilious
heads held high
the up stage stiff
pretentious guns
miss much that meets
my humbler eye
not that i meddle
perk or pry
but i m too small
to feel great pride
and as the pompous world
goes by
i see things from
the under side

above me wheel
the stars and suns
but humans shut

me from the sky
you see their eyes as pure
as nuns
i see their wayward
feet and sly
i own and own it with
a sigh
my point of view
is somewhat wried
i am a pessimistic
guy
i see things from the
under side

l envoi
prince ere you pull a bluff
and lie
before you fake
and play the snide
consider whether
archy s nigh
i see things from
the under side

Factory Windows Are Always Broken

Factory windows are always broken.
Somebody's always throwing bricks,
Somebody's always heaving cinders,
Playing ugly Yahoo tricks.

Factory windows are always broken.
Other windows are let alone.
No one throws through the chapel-window
The bitter, snarling, derisive stone.

Factory windows are always broken.
Something or other is going wrong.
Something is rotten—I think, in Denmark.
End of the factory-window song.

A Colloquial Reply: To Any Newsboy

If you lay for Iago at the stage door with a brick
You have missed the moral of the play.
He will have a midnight supper with Othello and his
  wife.
They will chirp together and be gay.

But the things Iago stands for must go down into the
    dust:
Lying and suspicion and conspiracy and lust.
And I cannot hate the Kaiser (I hope you understand.)
Yet I chase the thing he stands for with a brickbat in my
    hand.

Niagara

I

Within the town of Buffalo
Are prosy men with leaden eyes.
Like ants they worry to and fro,
(Important men, in Buffalo.)
But only twenty miles away
A deathless glory is at play:
Niagara, Niagara.

The women buy their lace and cry:—
"O such a delicate design,"
And over ostrich feathers sigh,
By counters there, in Buffalo.
The children haunt the trinket shops,
They buy false-faces, bells, and tops,
Forgetting great Niagara.

Within the town of Buffalo
Are stores with garnets, sapphires, pearls,
Rubies, emeralds aglow,—
Opal chains in Buffalo,

Cherished symbols of success.
They value not your rainbow dress:—
Niagara, Niagara.

The shaggy meaning of her name
This Buffalo, this recreant town,
Sharps and lawyers prune and tame:
Few pioneers in Buffalo;
Except young lovers flushed and fleet
And winds hallooing down the street:
"Niagara, Niagara."

The journalists are sick of ink:
Boy prodigals are lost in wine,
By night where white and red lights blink,
The eyes of Death, in Buffalo.
And only twenty miles away
Are starlit rocks and healing spray:—
Niagara, Niagara.

Above the town a tiny bird,
A shining speck at sleepy dawn,
Forgets the ant-hill so absurd,
This self-important Buffalo.
Descending twenty miles away
He bathes his wings at break of day—
Niagara, Niagara.

What marching men of Buffalo
Flood the streets in rash crusade?
Fools-to-free-the-world, they go,
Primeval hearts from Buffalo.
Red cataracts of France today
Awake, three thousand miles away
An echo of Niagara,
The cataract Niagara.

Kalamazoo

Once, in the city of Kalamazoo,
The gods went walking, two and two,
With the friendly phœnix, the stars of Orion,
The speaking pony and singing lion.
For in Kalamazoo in a cottage apart
Lived the girl with the innocent heart.
Thenceforth the city of Kalamazoo
Was the envied, intimate chum of the sun.
He rose from a cave by the principal street.
The lions sang, the dawn-horns blew,
And the ponies danced on silver feet.
He hurled his clouds of love around;
Deathless colors of his old heart
Draped the houses and dyed the ground.
O shrine of that wide young Yankee land,
Incense city of Kalamazoo,
That held, in the midnight, the priceless sun
As a jeweller holds an opal in hand!

From the awkward city of Oshkosh came
Love, (the bully no whip shall tame),
Bringing his gang of sinners bold.
And I was the least of his Oshkosh men;
But none were reticent, none were old.
And we joined the singing phœnix then,
And shook the lilies of Kalamazoo
All for one hidden butterfly.
Bulls of glory, in cars of war
We charged the boulevards, proud to die
For her ribbon sailing there on high.
Our blood set gutters all aflame,
Where the sun slept without any shame,
Cold rock till he must rise again.
She made great poets of wolf-eyed men—
The dear queen-bee of Kalamazoo,
With her crystal wings, and her honey heart.
We fought for her favors a year and a day
(Oh, the bones of the dead, the Oshkosh dead,
That were scattered along her pathway red!)
And then, in her harum-scarum way,
She left with a passing traveller-man—
With a singing Irishman
Went to Japan.

Why do the lean hyenas glare
Where the glory of Artemis had begun—
Of Atalanta, Joan of Arc,
Lorna Doone, Rosy O'Grady,
And Orphant Annie all in one?
Who burned this city of Kalamazoo

Till nothing was left but a ribbon or two—
One scorched phœnix that mourned in the dew,
Acres of ashes, a junk-man's cart,
A torn-up letter, a dancing shoe
(And the bones of the valiant dead)?
Who burned this city of Kalamazoo—
Love-town Troy-town Kalamazoo?

A harum-scarum innocent heart.

FRANKLIN P. ADAMS | 1881–1960

Us Potes

Swift was sweet on Stella;
   Poe had his Lenore;
Burns's fancy turned to Nancy
   And a dozen more.

Pope was quite a trifler;
   Goldsmith was a case;
Byron'd flirt with any skirt
   From Liverpool to Thrace.

Sheridan philandered;
   Shelley, Keats, and Moore
All were there with some affair
   Far from lit'rachoor.

Fickle is the heart of
   Each immortal bard.
Mine alone is made of stone—
   Gotta work too hard.

Ballade of Schopenhauer's Philosophy

Wishful to add to my mental power,
   Avid of knowledge and wisdom, I
Pondered the Essays of Schopenhauer,
   Taking his terrible hills on high.
   Worried I was, and a trifle shy,
Fearful I'd find him a bit opaque!
   Thus does he say, with a soul-sick sigh:
"The best you get is an even break."

Life, he says, is awry and sour;
   Life, he adds, is sour and awry;
Love, he says, is a withered flower;
   Love, he adds, is a dragon-fly;
   Love, he swears, is the Major Lie;
Life, he vows, is the Great Mistake;
   No one can beat it, and few can tie.
The best you get is an even break.

Women, he says, are clouds that lower;
   Women dissemble and falsify.
(Those are things that The Conning Tower
   Cannot asseverate or deny.)
   Futile to struggle, and strain, and try;
Pleasure is freedom from pain and ache;
   The greatest thing you can do is die—
The best you get is an even break.

Gosh! I feel like a real good cry!
   Life, he says, is a cheat, a fake.
Well, I agree with the grouchy guy—
   The best you get is an even break.

The Rich Man

The rich man has his motor-car,
   His country and his town estate.
He smokes a fifty-cent cigar
      And jeers at Fate.

He frivols through the livelong day,
   He knows not Poverty, her pinch.
His lot seems light, his heart seems gay;
      He has a cinch.

Yet though my lamp burns low and dim,
   Though I must slave for livelihood—
Think you that I would change with him?
      You bet I would!

To a Thesaurus

O precious codex, volume, tome,
   Book, writing, compilation, work
Attend the while I pen a pome,
   A jest, a jape, a quip, a quirk.

For I would pen, engross, indite,
  Transcribe, set forth, compose, address,
Record, submit—yea, even write
  An ode, an elegy to bless—

To bless, set store by, celebrate,
  Approve, esteem, endow with soul,
Commend, acclaim, appreciate,
  Immortalize, laud, praise, extol.

Thy merit, goodness, value, worth,
  Expedience, utility—
O manna, honey, salt of earth,
  I sing, I chant, I worship thee!

How could I manage, live, exist,
  Obtain, produce, be real, prevail,
Be present in the flesh, subsist,
  Have place, become, breathe or inhale,

Without thy help, recruit, support,
  Opitulation, furtherance,
Assistance, rescue, aid, resort,
  Favor, sustention, and advance?

Alas! alack! and well-a-day!
  My case would then be dour and sad,
Likewise distressing, dismal, gray,
  Pathetic, mournful, dreary, bad.

Though I could keep this up all day,
   This lyric, elegiac song,
Meseems hath come the time to say
   Farewell! adieu! good-by! so long!

"Lines Where Beauty Lingers"

From "Index of First Lines" In THE HOME BOOK OF VERSE

Tell me not, Sweet, I am unkind
That which her slender waist confined
It fell about the Martinmas
Out of the clover and blue-eyed grass

A fool there was and he made his prayer
A flying word from here and there
It is not, Celia, in our power
I've watched you now a full half-hour

O, my luve's like a red, red rose
Love is a sickness full of woes
Balkis was in her marble town
Ay, tear her tattered ensign down!

At setting day and rising morn
She stood breast high among the corn
My heart leaps up when I behold
Ben Battle was a soldier bold

A child should always say what's true
I am his Highness' dog at Kew
By the rude bridge that arched the flood
A ruddy drop of manly blood

A little Boy was set to keep
Day set on Norham's castle steep
Ah, did you once see Shelley plain?
Give me more love, or more disdain

Love in my bosom like a bee
Love still has something of the sea
I sat with one I love last night
She was a phantom of delight

An Immorality

Sing we for love and idleness,
Naught else is worth the having.

Though I have been in many a land,
There is naught else in living.

And I would rather have my sweet,
Though rose-leaves die of grieving,

Than do high deeds in Hungary
To pass all men's believing.

Ancient Music

Winter is icummen in,
Lhude sing Goddamm,
Raineth drop and staineth slop,
And how the wind doth ramm!
                              Sing: Goddamm.
Skiddeth bus and sloppeth us,
An ague hath my ham.

Freezeth river, turneth liver,
                    Damn you, sing: Goddamm.
Goddamm, Goddamm, 'tis why I am, Goddamm,
                    So 'gainst the winter's balm.
Sing goddamm, damm, sing Goddamm,
Sing goddamm, sing goddamm, DAMM.

T. S. ELIOT | 1888–1965

The Naming of Cats

The Naming of Cats is a difficult matter,
    It isn't just one of your holiday games;
You may think at first I'm as mad as a hatter
When I tell you, a cat must have THREE DIFFERENT
      NAMES.
First of all, there's the name that the family use daily,
    Such as Peter, Augustus, Alonzo or James,
Such as Victor or Jonathan, George or Bill Bailey—
    All of them sensible everyday names.
There are fancier names if you think they sound
      sweeter.
    Some for the gentlemen, some for the dames:
Such as Plato, Admetus, Electra, Demeter—
    But all of them sensible everyday names.
But: I tell you, a cat needs a name that's particular,
    A name that's peculiar, and more dignified,
Else how can he keep up his tail perpendicular,
    Or spread out his whiskers, or cherish his pride?
Of names of this kind, I can give you a quorum,
    Such as Munkustrap, Quaxo, or Coricopat,
Such as Bombalurina, or else Jellylorum—
    Names that never belong to more than one cat.
But above and beyond there's still one name left over,
    And that is the name that you never will guess;

The name that no human research can discover—
    But THE CAT HIMSELF KNOWS, and will never confess.
When you notice a cat in profound meditation,
    The reason, I tell you, is always the same:
His mind is engaged in a rapt contemplation
    Of the thought, of the thought, of the thought of his
        name:
      His ineffable effable
      Effanineffable
Deep and inscrutable singular Name.

Macavity: The Mystery Cat

Macavity's a Mystery Cat: he's called the Hidden Paw—
For he's the master criminal who can defy the Law.
He's the bafflement of Scotland Yard, the Flying Squad's
    despair:
For when they reach the scene of crime—*Macavity's not
    there!*

Macavity, Macavity, there's no one like Macavity,
He's broken every human law, he breaks the law of gravity.
His powers of levitation would make a fakir stare,
And when you reach the scene of crime—*Macavity's not
    there!*
You may seek him in the basement, you may look up in
    the air—
But I tell you once and once again, *Macavity's not there!*

Macavity's a ginger cat, he's very tall and thin;
You would know him if you saw him, for his eyes are
    sunken in.
His brow is deeply lined with thought, his head is highly
    domed;
His coat is dusty from neglect, his whiskers are
    uncombed.
He sways his head from side to side, with movements
    like a snake;
And when you think he's half asleep, he's always wide
    awake.

Macavity, Macavity, there's no one like Macavity,
For he's a fiend in feline shape, a monster of depravity.
You may meet him in a by-street, you may see him in
    the square—
But when a crime's discovered, then *Macavity's not there!*

He's outwardly respectable. (They say he cheats at
    cards.)
And his footprints are not found in any file of Scotland
    Yard's.
And when the larder's looted, or the jewel-case is rifled,
Or when the milk is missing, or another Peke's been
    stifled,
Or the greenhouse glass is broken, and the trellis past
    repair—
Ay, there's the wonder of the thing! *Macavity's not there!*

And when the Foreign Office find a Treaty's gone astray,
Or the Admiralty lose some plans and drawings by the
way.
There may be a scrap of paper in the hall or on the
stair—
But it's useless to investigate—*Macavity's not there!*
And when the loss has been disclosed, the Secret Service
say:
'It *must* have been Macavity!'—but he's a mile away.
You'll be sure to find him resting, or a-licking of his
thumbs,
Or engaged in doing complicated long division sums.

Macavity, Macavity, there's no one like Macavity,
There never was a Cat of such deceitfulness and suavity.
He always has an alibi, and one or two to spare:
At whatever time the deed took place—MACAVITY
WASN'T THERE!
And they say that all the Cats whose wicked deeds are
widely known
(I might mention Mungojerrie, I might mention Griddle-
bone)
Are nothing more than agents for the Cat who all the
time
Just controls their operations: the Napoleon of Crime!

Tannhauser

While strolling through the hills one day,
In search of joy and laughter,
Tannhauser, in his travels, came
Upon a flat run by a dame
Who said that Venus was her name;
At least so he said after.
Tannhauser said, "I like it here.
I think I'll stick around a year."

Tannhauser liked the place a lot;
He thought the girls entrancing,
And Venus entertained him so
He quite forgot he had to go.
They even ran a burlesque show,
With lots of songs and dancing.
(They pulled a dance of nymphs and satyrs
That wouldn't do in most theaytres.)

I can't tell all the things they did
(The censor would delete it)
Until our hero said, "I hate
To go so soon. It's getting late,
I quite forgot I have a date;
I guess I gotta beat it.

I've had a lovely time, old wren."
And Venus said, "Call soon again."

Tannhauser had a girl named Bess,
Her old man ran a glee club.
Our hero, passing by the place
That afternoon, came face to face
With Pa, returning from the chase,
Who said, "Come, visit *the* club.
We're running off a singing fest.
He weds my girl who sings the best."

A baritone named Wolfram
Started off the show quite gayly.
Tann looked at Bess and chuckled low,
"This Wolfram guy don't stand no show.
He couldn't book with Marcus Loew."
And tuned his ukulele.
"This lieder stuff don't make a hit,
I think I'll jazz it up a bit."

He bowed politely to the gang.
The following's the song he sang:
"These Wartburg janes don't go with me,
Gimme a kid with pep.
I know one that has it,
She knows how to jazz it,
Venus is the baby that can teach 'em how to step.
So strike up a tune on the old trombone.
Play that haunting solo on the saxophone,
Put your arms around her waist and kick up your shoes,

Dancing with your Venus,
Prancing with your Venus,
Doing those Venusberg Blues."

The Wartburg boys got sore as pups,
And said, "Who let that guy in?
He sure has got a lot of gall
To pull that stuff around this hall.
Let's throw him off the castle wall,
Or punch his blooming eye in."
But Bess said, "No, boys, let it pass.
The lad ain't used to mix with class."

Tannhauser, feeling quite put out,
To go to Rome decided.
Returning in a year or less
He said, "I think I'll call on Bess
And square myself with her. I guess
No gent would act like I did."
But Bess's grief has made her croak.
That girl could never take a joke.

Tannhauser said, "Well, that ends that.
Since all is o'er between us
This Wartburg joint is far from gay,
I'm lonesome for the Great White Way,
I think I'll call this day a day
And telephone to Venus.
That little French kid was a bear;
I wonder if that blonde's still there."

A band of pilgrims passing by,
Returning from an outing,
Said, "Listen, bo, don't give up hope;
We've been to Rome to see the Pope,
We're handing you the latest dope:
His staff has started sprouting."
Tannhauser said, "Oh, is that so!"
And died. I think it's some fool show.

Carmen

In Spain, where the courtly Castilian hidalgo twangs
     lightly each night his romantic guitar,
Where the castanets clink on the gay piazetta, and
     strains of fandangoes are heard from afar,
There lived, I am told, a bold hussy named Carmen, a
     pampered young vamp full of devil and guile.
Cigarette and cigar men were smitten with Carmen;
     from near and from far men were caught with her
     smile.
Now one day it happened she got in a scrap and
     proceeded to beat up a girl in the shop,
Till someone suggested they have her arrested, and
     though she protested they called in a cop.
In command of the guard was a shavetail named José, a
     valiant young don with a weakness for janes,
And so great was her beauty this bold second loot he
     could not do his duty and put her in chains.
"I'm sorry, my dear, to appear to arrest you,—at best
     you are hardly much more than a kid.

If I let you go, say, there'll be some exposé. But beat it,"
     said José. And beat it she did.

The scene now is changed to a strange sort of tavern—a
     hangout of gypsies, a rough kind of dive,

And Carmen, who *can* sing, is warbling and dancing,
     awaiting her date the late loot to arrive.

In comes Escamillo the toreadoro and sings his great
     solo 'mid plaudits and cheers,

And when he concludes, after three or four encores, the
     gypsies depart and Don José appears.

These gypsy companions of Carmen are smugglers, the
     worst band of bandits and cut throats in Spain.

And José, we know well's A.W.O.L. Says he, "Since
     that's so, well I guess I'll remain."

The gypsies depart to the heart of the mountains, and
     with them goes José who's grouchy and sore.

For Carmen, the flirt, has deserted poor José, and
     transferred her love to the toreador.

And as he sits sulking he sees Escamillo. A challenge is
     passed and they draw out their knives.

Till José, though lighter, disarms the bull fighter and
     nears kills the blighter when Carmen arrives.

Now comes Micaela, Don José's young sweetheart, a
     nice looking blonde without much in her dome.

Says she, "Do you know, kid, your ma's kinder low,
     kid?" Says José, "Let's go, kid," and follows her
     home.

At last we arrive at the day of the bull fight; the grand
     stand is packed and the bleachers are full;

A picturesque scene, a square near the arena, the Plaza
     del Toro or Place of the Bull.

Dark skinned senoritas with fans and mantillas, and
    haughty Castilians in festive array;
And dolled out to charm men, suspecting no harm,
    enters, last of all, Carmen to witness the fray.
But here's our friend José who seizes her bridle. A wild
    homicidal glint gleams in his eye.
He's mad and disgusted and cries out, "You've busted
    the heart that once trusted you. Wed me or die!"
Though Carmen is frightened at how this scene might
    end, I'm forced to admit she is game to the last.
She says to him, "Banish the notion and vanish. *Vamos!*"
    which is Spanish for "run away fast."
A scream and a struggle! She reels and she staggers, for
    Don José's dagger's plunged deep in her breast.
No more will she flirt in her old way, that's certain. So
    ring down the curtain, poor Carmen's at rest.

Rigoletto

Although some are afraid that to speak of a spade as a
    spade is a social mistake,
Yet there's none will dispute it was common repute that
    fair Mantua's Duke was a rake.
To continue the trope, Rigoletto, his fool,
Was a bit of a blade, but was more of a tool.

Rigoletto had hit with the barbs of his wit many
    prominent persons at court,
Till at last they combined, in their anger, to find a
    conclusive and fitting retort.

Which they found, as it chanced, in an opportune way
When they learned that he called on a girl every day.

Now the fool was devoted, it's proper to note, to his
    child,—his one passion in life,
A sweet maiden and fair who'd been left in his care by
    the early demise of his wife.
And this daughter named Gilda, he loved to a fault.
She'd a range from low G up to E flat in alt.

So one night, as they'd planned, the conspirator band
    stole the maiden away from her dad.
When she came from the street to the Duke's private
    suite she remarked, "Well, I guess I'm in bad."
    . . . I need mention no more,
For the Duke was a rake, as I told you before.
It is needless to add that the jester was mad when he
    heard of the fate of his child,
And he cried "Watch the fool knock the Duke for a
    gool!" and made other threats equally wild.

"Though I'm odd I'll be even!" he punned through his
    tears—
Broken hearted he clung to the habit of years.

So in anger he flew to a gunman he knew, an assassin
    residing quite near,
And agreed on a plan with this murderous man to
    conclude the Duke's earthly career.
"You'll be paid for your pains," the fool hastened to say.
"The more pains you inflict, so much greater your pay."

Now, this man had a sister, a buxom young miss, who
    when business was active and brisk,
Like a dutiful maid helped him out with the trade, and
    divided the profits and risk.
And it happened that night—call it luck or a fluke,
That this girl, Madeline, had a date with the Duke.

When she learned that the end of her gentleman friend
    had been scheduled to take place that night,
She exclaimed with a cry, "Brother, lay off that guy, for I
    don't think you're treating me right.
Gawd knows I'm no angel but somehow I hate
For to see a lad beaned the one time I've a date."

Then the murderer said "Well, I'll bump off instead the
    first stranger that comes to our place."
Madalena said "Great! Then I won't break my date."
    and proceeded to powder her face.
For in spite of her trade she was rather refined,
And extremely well bred for a girl of her kind.

At about ten o'clock came a diffident knock ('twas
    beginning to thunder and pour),
And there Gilda stood, clad in the garb of a lad, as the
    murderer came to the door.
So he stabbed her quite neatly three times in the back
And he wrapped up her corpse in an old burlap sack.

Rigoletto with glee paid the brigand his fee, then he
    dashed through the rain and the wind.
When he opened the sack he was taken aback, and
    exclaimed "I'm extremely chagrined.
I think that assassin deserves a rebuke
For he murdered my girl when I paid for a Duke."

Pelleas and Melisande

Compared with this a grave or tomb
Would seem extremely jolly.
This opus takes the prize for gloom
And dismal melancholy.
A most unhappy man, I think,
Must be the author, Maeterlinck.

Beside a dark, depressing pond,
While hunting to beguile him,
Prince Golo came on Melisande,
Just out of an asylum.
At least when she began to speak
'Twas clear her intellect was weak.

The maiden started with a cry,
Exclaiming, "Pray don't harm me."
Said Golo, "Be my bride for I
Am also slightly barmy.
I think you'll like my folks. In fact
My whole damned family is cracked."

I doubt if ever had a bride
A gloomier homecoming.
No sunlight reached the house. Beside
There wasn't any plumbing.
Said she, "A morgue would be more cheerful."
He answered, "Mel, you said an carful."

Their honeymoon was brief, alas,
For as the season wore on
She fell in love with Pelleas,
A handsome low grade moron;
Her husband's younger brother who,
Though witless, had the wit to woo.

At night she'd loose her golden hair
From out her window casement
To Pelly who was standing there
Downstairs, outside the basement.
And as he grabbed her silken tresses
He'd smother them with warm caresses.

They'd meet each other every day
In dank unpleasant places,
And in an imbecilic way
Indulge in chaste embraces.
And once, beside a dismal pool
She lost her wedding ring, the fool!

When Golo heard about the ring
(She thought he wouldn't mind it)
He raved and swore like anything,
And said, "Go out and find it."
With Pelleas she searched all night,
The poor simps didn't have a light.

At last it filtered through the bean
Of that poor half wit, Golo,
That Melisande's big third act scene
Was not exactly solo.
Said he, "My royal pride is hurt.
I fear my wife has done me dirt."

And so that night he found the two.
(By now he'd grown to hate her.)
His brother on the spot he slew,
His wife died sometime later.
For harmless fun and merry banter
Give *me* Ed Wynn or Eddie Cantor.

JOHN CROWE RANSOM | 1888–1974

Survey of Literature

In all the good Greek of Plato
I lack my roast beef and potato.

A better man was Aristotle,
Pulling steady on the bottle.

I dip my hat to Chaucer
Swilling soup from his saucer,

And to Master Shakespeare
Who wrote big on small beer.

The abstemious Wordsworth
Subsisted on a curd's-worth,

But a slick one was Tennyson,
Putting gravy on his venison.

What these men had to eat and drink
Is what we say and what we think.

The flatulence of Milton
Came out of wry Stilton.

Sing a song for Percy Shelley,
Drowned in pale lemon jelly,

And for precious John Keats,
Dripping blood of pickled beets.

Then there was poor Willie Blake,
He foundered on sweet cake.

God have mercy on the sinner
Who must write with no dinner,

No gravy and no grub,
No pewter and no pub,

No belly and no bowels,
Only consonants and vowels.

SAMUEL HOFFENSTEIN | 1890–1947

FROM **Love-songs, at Once Tender and Informative—An Unusual Combination in Verses of This Character**

Maid of Gotham, ere we part,
Have a hospitable heart—

Since our own delights must end,
Introduce me to your friend.

———

If you love me, as I love you,
We'll both be friendly and untrue.

———

Let us build a little house
With instalments, love and craft,
Fit for you, my precious mouse—
Garden fore and garden aft.

There we'll love and play (I hope)
Work, beget and dream (I trust)
Sweetly with such problems cope
As plague whatever stems of dust.

We shall have such rosy tryst;
Ours will be a blessed fate;
Love will daily grow (I wist)
So (D.G.) will real estate.

When the jealous powers above
Magic from our couplet steal,
We may then conclude our love
With a profitable deal.

———

My sanguine and adventurous dear,
Whom long experience taught no fear,
I shall make a ballad of
The repetitions of your love.

Every time you love again,
Former lovers failed in vain:
Your ardor rises like the sun
On the last and only one.

You but tell the simple truth
Out of your perennial youth;
When I sing of you, I sing
A heart whose every month is spring.

Marvellous unto my sight
Your quasi-virginal delight;
But dearer, sweeter, rarer yet,
How you remember to forget.

Bless your heart, that phœnix-wise,
Can from its amorous ashes rise:
The years their disappointments waste
On a memory so chaste.

———

Your little hands,
Your little feet,
Your little mouth—
Oh, God, how sweet!

Your little nose,
Your little ears,
Your eyes, that shed
Such little tears!

Your little voice,
So soft and kind;
Your little soul,
Your little mind!

———

Had we but parted at the start,
I'd cut some figure in your heart;
And though the lands between were wide,
You'd often see me at your side.

But having loved and stayed, my dear,
I'm always everywhere but here,
And, still more paradoxical,
You always see me not at all.

FROM The Notebook of a Schnook

schnook = schlemiel

I

I'm sitting home, I feel lonesome,
I feel saber-toothed and ownsome;
If I had a friend of the female gender
I feel I could make the girl surrender.
So I call this one, I call that one,
A bright one, a dim one, a slim one, a fat one,
Till I find a girl who says she's willing

To do the cooing if I do the billing.
So I bill in one place, I bill in another,
And she coos a little, like Whistler's mother;
Then I take her home to my mortgaged chalet,
A cute little place, if not a *palais*,
In a very respectable part of town,
With some rooms upstairs and some down;
I play a record by Tchaikovsky,
A very high-toned approach to lovsky;

    I play waltzes by all the Strausses
And name big names in adjoining houses;
I try etchings, book-ends, brandy,
Rare editions and nougat candy,
Broadloom carpet and rose-leaf ceiling,
On which she can look, I hope, with feeling—
And what happens? You won't believe it;
As usual, nothing—take it or leave it!

II

I write a scenario for moving pictures;
I let myself go without any strictures;
My mind works in bright ascensions;
The characters swell and get dimensions;
The heroine rises from Gimbel's basement
To what could be called a magic casement,
By sheer virtue and, call it pluck,
With maybe a reel and a half of luck;
She doesn't use posterior palsy
Or displace so much as a single falsie;
She scorns the usual oo-la-la
And never ruffles a modest bra,

(The censor's dream of the cinema);
She doesn't find pearls in common oysters;
She sips a little but never roisters.
The hero's gonads are under wraps,
He never clutches or cuffs or slaps
In heat Vesuvian, or even Stygian—
He acts Oxonian or Cantabrigian
With maybe a soupçon of the South—
Cotton wouldn't melt in his mouth;
The plot could harmlessly beguile
A William Wordsworth honey chile;
The Big Shot's hot and the little shotlets
Wake their wives with contagious hotlets.
So what happens? The usual factors—
The studio simply can't get actors,
Directors, cutters, stagehands, stages,
Or girls to type the extra pages:
The way it ends, to put it briefly,
Is what happens is nothing, chiefly.

FROM Poems in Praise of Practically Nothing

You leap out of bed; you start to get ready;
You dress and you dress till you feel unsteady;
Hours go by, and still you're busy
Putting on clothes, till your brain is dizzy.
Do you flinch? Do you quit? Do you go out naked?—
The least little button, you don't forsake it.
What thanks do you get? Well, for all this mess, yet
When night comes around, you've got to undress yet.

You're a good girl; you're gray with virtue;
The very thought of a misstep hurts you;
You know that honor must be hoarded
Against the day when it is rewarded;
You see a girl who's all men's vassal,
Marry a duke in his own castle;
You see another, who can't say, "No, sir,"
Capture, at least, a wholesale grocer;—
But you never let your thoughts grow sordid:
You know in your heart you'll be rewarded.
Well, the years go by, like queens and roses,
The way they did in the time of Moses,
And what do you get? False teeth, a doorman,
A complex, or assistant foreman!

You go to high school, even college;
You become a regular Book of Knowledge;
You learn that Nero played the fiddle;
That the Sphinx is, after all, a riddle;
That women weep while men go faring;
That Bismarck seldom was a herring.
No matter what a person asks you,
The brilliant answer never tasks you;
You smile and say, "Go ask another,"
Like, "Did the Gracchi have a mother?"
Well, you meet a girl, and nothing sweeter;

The kind—well, anyhow, you meet 'er—
You look her over with elation—
She seems to have a cerebration:
So you start right in, like Kipling's thunder,
To be the twenty-seventh wonder;
You spout such high and fancy learning,
You're sure the girl will die of yearning—
And when you're finished, did you please her?
Did you hear her say, "You're Julius Caesar"?
What thanks did you get? The usual solo:
She likes the Prince of Wales and polo.

FROM **Songs About Life and Brighter Things Yet;
A Survey of the Entire Earthly Panorama,
Animal, Vegetable and Mineral, with
Appropriate Comment by the Author, of a
Philosophic, Whimsical, Humorous or Poetic
Nature — a Truly Remarkable Undertaking**

The serpent has no feet or hands,
Yet makes his way in many lands;
But who would on his belly crawl
In order to avoid a fall?

———

Though Cæsar stop a bunghole now,
With no green myrtle on his brow,
Remember, ere you shake your head

So wisely, that friend Cæsar's dead.
He does not stop, with mind and shin
And heart and occiput and chin,
The kicks and cuffs the fates bestow
On all who linger here below.
I'm sure, his dust he would not barter
For any living bunghole-starter.

———

The crickets chirping in the dark;
The glow-worms with their sudden spark;
I like the sturdy hills that rise
In gracious worship of the skies;
The grove, the field, the church-like wood,
The sweet, adventurous solitude.
I like to watch the cattle graze
Silent in the sunny days:
The cows, that waking seem to sleep;
The woolly and untroubled sheep,
So simple and so unaware
They seem to blend into the air.
And yet I should be quite cast down
To see the country come to town.
I like the country best for this;—
Because they put it where it is.

The Sexes

The sexes aren't very nice:
They are but instruments of vice.

If the obscure amoeba can
Get on without them, so should Man.

The dwellers in the pure serene
Are scrupulously epicene.

They play a little music, yes,
But merely out of blessedness.

Of course the Latin peoples are
Morally crepuscular.

But the Nordic will inherit
Heaven and earth for special merit.

A race so nobly destined ought
To propagate by power of thought—

Which the exalted Nordic can
More nearly do than any man.

For nothing is, as well you know,
But constant thinking makes it so.

CHRISTOPHER MORLEY | 1890–1957

Elegy Written in a Country Coal-Bin

The furnace tolls the knell of falling steam,
   The coal supply is virtually done,
And at this price, indeed it does not seem
   As though we could afford another ton.

Now fades the glossy, cherished anthracite;
   The radiators lose their temperature:
How ill avail, on such a frosty night,
   The "short and simple flannels of the poor."

Though in the icebox, fresh and newly laid,
   The rude forefathers of the omelet sleep,
No eggs for breakfast till the bill is paid:
   We cannot cook again till coal is cheap.

Can Morris-chair or papier-mâché bust
   Revivify the failing pressure-gauge?
Chop up the grand piano if you must,
   And burn the East Aurora parrot-cage!

Full many a can of purest kerosene
   The dark unfathomed tanks of Standard Oil
Shall furnish me, and with their aid I mean
   To bring my morning coffee to a boil.

A Pre-Raphaelite
Had to have things right.
The patient redhead, Elizabeth Siddal,
Lay in the bathtub up to her middle
(But richly gowned)
To show what she would look like drowned.
At last she sneezed: Oh Mr. Millais,
Do I 'ave to welter 'ere all day?
It's enough to congeal ya:
Posing for Ophelia.

MAXWELL BODENHEIM | 1892–1954

Upper Family

In Nineteen Hundred they preferred
Parchesi, lottoes, and charades.
The ladies two-stepped, barely stirred.
The men sneaked down to Bowery shades
And filled their stove-pipe hats with beer,
Drank them in one gulp, won the bets
And in the ragtime, frowsy cheer,
Berated corsets and lorgnettes.
The ladies with a smattering
Of French, discussed—in murmured quips—
The Marquis who was scattering
Moustache-imprints on many lips.
On Saturdays the family rode
In liveried broughams, satirized
The World's Fair aftermath, the mode
Ta-ra-ra-boom-deeayed, vulgarized.
Art served them as an interlude,
Grand Opera in florid tones,
Or paintings where a seated nude
Aroused frustrated, hidden groans.
The men were brokers, juggled stocks,
Played a hard game in market-hives.
With hearts as merciless as clocks
They timed the death of distant lives.

One lady in her youth found sex
In ways devious and plentiful.
Then she concealed the blackmail cheques
Through married days respected, dull.
This family honored its own kind.
Here favors could not be refused.
Others were treated like the blind —
Inferior souls born to be used.
But now the sons and daughters tryst
With horror, maddening *coup d'état*.
A son became a Socialist —
They buried him with sweet éclat.
He could not bear the family's veiled
Assumption of nobility,
While men with conscience were assailed
As bores above servility.
They buried him, but still his full
Street-pacing ghost pollutes the air,
And in nightmares they see him pull
A rickshaw at the next World Fair.

EDNA ST. VINCENT MILLAY | 1892–1950

First Fig

My candle burns at both ends;
   It will not last the night;
But ah, my foes, and oh, my friends —
   It gives a lovely light!

Second Fig

Safe upon the solid rock the ugly houses stand:
Come and see my shining palace built upon the sand!

Thursday

And if I loved you Wednesday,
   Well, what is that to you?
I do not love you Thursday—
   So much is true.

And why you come complaining
   Is more than I can see.
I loved you Wednesday,—yes—but what
   Is that to me?

Grown-Up

Was it for this I uttered prayers,
And sobbed and cursed and kicked the stairs,
That now, domestic as a plate,
I should retire at half-past eight?

MORRIS BISHOP | 1893–1973

Ozymandias Revisited

I met a traveller from an antique land
Who said: Two vast and trunkless legs of stone
Stand in the desert. Near them on the sand,
Half sunk, a shatter'd visage lies, whose frown
And wrinkled lip and sneer of cold command
Tell that its sculptor well those passions read
Which yet survive, stamp'd on these lifeless things,
The hand that mock'd them and the heart that fed;
And on the pedestal these words appear:
"My name is Ozymandias, king of kings:
Look on my works, ye Mighty, and despair!"
Also the names of Emory P. Gray,
Mr. and Mrs. Dukes, and Oscar Baer
Of 17 West 4th St., Oyster Bay.

Eschatology

I have no care for Systematic Theology,
But oh, the recurrent hour of bile that brings
Fainness for specialization in Eschatology
(Greek, you recall, for the study of all Last Things)!

Come, day when the wealth of the world is less than
    tuppence,
The seas unfretted, and the monuments down,
When the proud have got their ultimate come-uppance,
And on the seventh New York the sand lies brown:

And all my sloth and failure, all my passion
One with the sorrow of the Gaul and Goth,
And all our fireproof homes are burnt and ashen,
And in the moth-proof closets dwells the moth;

And every most unspeakable thing is spoken,
Rust in the rust-resisting pipes of brass,
And all unbreakable things at last are broken;
Shatter'd the non-shatterable glass.

We Have Been Here Before

I think I remember this moorland,
    The tower on the tip of the tor;
I feel in the distance another existence;
    I think I have been here before.

And I think you were sitting beside me
    In a fold in the face of the fell;
For Time at its work'll go round in a circle,
    And what is befalling, befell.

"I have been here before!" I asserted,
    In a nook on a neck of the Nile.
I once in a crisis was punished by Isis,
    And you smiled. I remember your smile.

I had the same sense of persistence
    On the site of the seat of the Sioux;
I heard in the teepee the sound of a sleepy
    Pleistocene grunt. It was you.

The past made a promise, before it
    Began to begin to begone.
This limited gamut brings you again. Damn it,
    How long has this got to go on?

———

A joker who haunts Monticello
Is really a terrible fellow;
    In the midst of caresses
    He fills ladies' dresses
With garter-snakes, ice-cubes, and jell-o.

Flowers of Rhetoric

I grant you there is much excuse
    For simile and metaphor,
But moderation in their use
    I'd wage a small vendetta for.

They gleam amid the puffing prose
   Of Art's advanced minorities
(As on the maiden's bosom glows
   The symbol of sororities

(Which bind with bonds like linkèd brass
   (As sturdy as austerity
(Which irritates like mustard gas
   (Which spreads like insincerity

(Elusive as a synonym
   (Which flees away like Saracens
(Who fought in battles vague and dim
   As most of these comparisons.))))))))

So everything's like something else
   In these new-fangled rhetorics.
But I'll resist 'em (like the Celts
   And hopeless Vercingetorix).

Ah, To Be In . . .

Ah to be in Rarotonga, 'neath the languor-laden breeze,
Or to be in Erromango, in the far New Hebrides!
Ah, to drowze beneath the palm trees on a green Pacific
   isle,
Where every prospect pleases and where man, besides,
   is vile!

There is magic in the atlas; how the names allure my
  eyes!
Ah, to be in Hiddi Birra, where the Jam-jam Mountains
  rise!
Or Kasongo on the Kongo, where Kibombo gleams
  afar!
Or in Kilwa Kisiwami, looking north to Zanzibar!

Oh, this life is dull and dreary; I would journey far away
To Jalalabad and Lhasa, to Kabul and Mandalay!
Ah, the Runn of Cutch! Rajpipla! and that dim and
  ancient land
Where the caravans come shuffling into silken
  Samarkand!

(There's a lad in old Rajpipla with an atlas in his clutch,
And his dreaming eyes are gazing far beyond the Runn
  of Cutch,
And mysterious music lures him, and he murmurs soft
  and low,
"Cincinnati! Cincinnati! Buffalo, ah, Buffalo!

"Ah, to be in that far city, blooming like a tropic rose,
Where by golden Allegheny the Monongahela flows;
How sweet the limpid syllables that stir my heart to joy,
As I whisper, 'Ah, Chicago! Fair Chicago, Illinois!' ")

Portrait of the Artist

Oh, lead me to a quiet cell
   Where never footfall rankles,
And bar the window passing well,
   And gyve my wrists and ankles.

Oh, wrap my eyes with linen fair,
   With hempen cord go bind me,
And, of your mercy, leave me there,
   Nor tell them where to find me.

Oh, lock the portal as you go,
   And see its bolts be double. . . .
Come back in half an hour or so,
   And I will be in trouble.

Chant for Dark Hours

   Some men, some men
   Cannot pass a
   Book shop.
(Lady, make your mind up, and wait your life away.)

Some men, some men
Cannot pass a
Crap game.
(He said he'd come at moonrise, and here's another
    day!)

Some men, some men
Cannot pass a
Bar-room.
(Wait about, and hang about, and that's the way it goes.)

Some men, some men
Cannot pass a
Woman.
(Heaven never send me another one of those!)

Some men, some men
Cannot pass a
Golf course.
(Read a book, and sew a seam, and slumber if you can.)

Some men, some men
Cannot pass a
Haberdasher's.
(All your life you wait around for some damn man!)

Unfortunate Coincidence

By the time you swear you're his,
    Shivering and sighing,
And he vows his passion is
    Infinite, undying—
Lady, make a note of this:
    One of you is lying.

Comment

Oh, life is a glorious cycle of song,
A medley of extemporanea;
And love is a thing that can never go wrong;
And I am Marie of Roumania.

Words of Comfort to be Scratched on a Mirror

Helen of Troy had a wandering glance;
Sappho's restriction was only the sky;
Ninon was ever the chatter of France;
But oh, what a good girl am I!

News Item

Men seldom make passes
At girls who wear glasses.

Song of One of the Girls

Here in my heart I am Helen;
    I'm Aspasia and Hero, at least.
I'm Judith, and Jael, and Madame de Staël;
    I'm Salomé, moon of the East.

Here in my soul I am Sappho;
    Lady Hamilton am I, as well.
In me Récamier vies with Kitty O'Shea,
    With Dido, and Eve, and poor Nell.

I'm of the glamorous ladies
    At whose beckoning history shook.
But you are a man, and see only my pan,
    So I stay at home with a book.

Fighting Words

Say my love is easy had,
    Say I'm bitten raw with pride,
Say I am too often sad,—
    Still behold me at your side.

Say I'm neither brave nor young,
    Say I woo and coddle care,
Say the devil touched my tongue,—
    Still you have my heart to wear.

But say my verses do not scan,
    And I get me another man!

Inscription for the Ceiling of a Bedroom

Daily dawns another day;
I must up, to make my way.
Though I dress and drink and eat,
Move my fingers and my feet,
Learn a little, here and there,
Weep and laugh and sweat and swear,
Hear a song, or watch a stage,
Leave some words upon a page,
Claim a foe, or hail a friend—
Bed awaits me at the end.

Though I go in pride and strength,
I'll come back to bed at length.
Though I walk in blinded woe,
Back to bed I'm bound to go.
High my heart, or bowed my head,
All my days but lead to bed.
Up, and out, and on; and then
Ever back to bed again,
Summer, Winter, Spring, and Fall—
I'm a fool to rise at all!

Experience

Some men break your heart in two,
    Some men fawn and flatter,
Some men never look at you;
    And that cleans up the matter.

Neither Bloody Nor Bowed

They say of me, and so they should,
It's doubtful if I come to good.
I see acquaintances and friends
Accumulating dividends,
And making enviable names
In science, art, and parlor games.
But I, despite expert advice,
Keep doing things I think are nice,
And though to good I never come—
Inseparable my nose and thumb!

Bohemia

Authors and actors and artists and such
Never know nothing, and never know much.
Sculptors and singers and those of their kidney
Tell their affairs from Seattle to Sydney.
Playwrights and poets and such horses' necks

Start off from anywhere, end up at sex.
Diarists, critics, and similar roe
Never say nothing, and never say no.
People Who Do Things exceed my endurance;
God, for a man that solicits insurance!

Story

"And if he's gone away," said she,
"Good riddance, if you're asking me.
I'm not a one to lie awake
And weep for anybody's sake.
There's better lads than him about!
I'll wear my buckled slippers out
A-dancing till the break of day.
I'm better off with him away!
And if he never come," said she,
"Now what on earth is that to me?
I wouldn't have him back!"
                              I hope
Her mother washed her mouth with soap.

Frustration

If I had a shiny gun,
I could have a world of fun
Speeding bullets through the brains
Of the folk who give me pains;

Or had I some poison gas,
I could make the moments pass
Bumping off a number of
People whom I do not love.

But I have no lethal weapon—
Thus does Fate our pleasure step on!
So they still are quick and well
Who should be, by rights, in hell.

Résumé

Razors pain you;
Rivers are damp;
Acids stain you;
And drugs cause cramp.
Guns aren't lawful;
Nooses give;
Gas smells awful;
You might as well live.

One Perfect Rose

A single flow'r he sent me, since we met.
    All tenderly his messenger he chose;
Deep-hearted, pure, with scented dew still wet—
    One perfect rose.

I knew the language of the floweret;
    "My fragile leaves," it said, "his heart enclose."
Love long has taken for his amulet
    One perfect rose.

Why is it no one ever sent me yet
    One perfect limousine, do you suppose?
Ah no, it's always just my luck to get
    One perfect rose.

Ballade at Thirty-Five

This, no song of an ingénue,
    This, no ballad of innocence;
This, the rhyme of a lady who
    Followed ever her natural bents.
    This, a solo of sapience,
This, a chantey of sophistry,
    This, the sum of experiments,—
I loved them until they loved me.

Decked in garments of sable hue,
    Daubed with ashes of myriad Lents,
Wearing shower bouquets of rue,
    Walk I ever in penitence.
    Oft I roam, as my heart repents,
Through God's acre of memory,
    Marking stones, in my reverence,
"I loved them until they loved me."

Pictures pass me in long review,—
    Marching columns of dead events.
I was tender, and, often, true;
    Ever a prey to coincidence.
    Always knew I the consequence;
Always saw what the end would be.
    We're as Nature has made us—hence
I loved them until they loved me.

L'ENVOI:

Princes, never I'd give offense,
    Won't you think of me tenderly?
Here's my strength and my weakness, gents,—
    I loved them until they loved me.

Healed

Oh, when I flung my heart away,
    The year was at its fall.
I saw my dear, the other day,
    Beside a flowering wall;
And this was all I had to say:
    "I thought that he was tall!"

Pour Prendre Congé

I'm sick of embarking in dories
    Upon an emotional sea.
I'm wearied of playing Dolores
    (A role never written for me).

I'll never again like a cub lick
    My wounds while I squeal at the hurt.
No more I'll go walking in public,
    My heart hanging out of my shirt.

I'm tired of entwining me garlands
    Of weather-worn hemlock and bay.
I'm over my longing for far lands—
    I wouldn't give that for Cathay.

I'm through with performing the ballet
    Of love unrequited and told.
Euterpe, I tender you *vale*;
    Good-by, and take care of that cold.

I'm done with this burning and giving
    And reeling the rhymes of my woes.
And how I'll be making my living,
    The Lord in His mystery knows.

Coda

There's little in taking or giving,
    There's little in water or wine;
This living, this living, this living
    Was never a project of mine.
Oh, hard is the struggle, and sparse is
    The gain of the one at the top,
For art is a form of catharsis,
    And love is a permanent flop,
And work is the province of cattle,
    And rest's for a clam in a shell,
So I'm thinking of throwing the battle—
    Would you kindly direct me to hell?

The Danger of Writing Defiant Verse

And now I have another lad!
    No longer need you tell
How all my nights are slow and sad
    For loving you too well.

His ways are not your wicked ways,
    He's not the like of you.
He treads his path of reckoned days,
    A sober man, and true.

They'll never see him in the town,
    Another on his knee.
He'd cut his laden orchards down,
    If that would pleasure me.

He'd give his blood to paint my lips,
    If I should wish them red.
He prays to touch my finger-tips
    Or stroke my prideful head.

He never weaves a glinting lie,
    Or brags the hearts he'll keep.
I have forgotten how to sigh—
    Remembered how to sleep.

He's none to kiss away my mind—
    A slower way is his.
Oh, Lord! On reading this, I find
    A silly lot he is.

The Actress

Her name, cut clear upon this marble cross,
    Shines, as it shone when she was still on earth;
While tenderly the mild, agreeable moss
    Obscures the figures of her date of birth.

the way to hump a cow is not
to get yourself a stool
but draw a line around the spot
and call it beautifool

to multiply because and why
dividing thens by nows
and adding and(i understand)
is hows to hump a cows

the way to hump a cow is not
to elevate your tool
but drop a penny in the slot
and bellow like a bool

to lay a wreath from ancient greath
on insulated brows
(while tossing boms at uncle toms)
is hows to hump a cows

the way to hump a cow is not
to push and then to pull
but practicing the art of swot
to preach the golden rull

to vote for me(all decent mem
and wonens will allows
which if they don't to hell with them)
is hows to hump a cows

F. SCOTT FITZGERALD | 1896–1940

Obit on Parnassus

Death before forty's no bar. Lo!
  These had accomplished their feats:
Chatterton, Burns, and Kit Marlowe,
  Byron and Shelley and Keats.

Death, the eventual censor,
  Lays for the forties, and so
Took off Jane Austen and Spenser,
  Stevenson, Hood, and poor Poe.

You'll leave a better-lined wallet
  By reaching the end of your rope
After fifty, like Shakespeare and Smollett,
  Thackeray, Dickens, and Pope.

Try for the sixties—but say, boy,
  That's when the tombstones were built on
Butler and Sheridan, the play boy,
  Arnold and Coleridge and Milton.

Three score and ten—the tides rippling
  Over the bar; slip the hawser.
Godspeed to Clemens and Kipling,
  Swinburne and Browning and Chaucer.

Some staved the debt off but paid it
    At eighty—that's after the law.
Wordsworth and Tennyson made it,
    And Meredith, Hardy, and Shaw.

But, Death, while you make up your quota,
    Please note this confession of candor—
That I wouldn't give an iota
    To linger till ninety, like Landor.

Sportif

Prescott, press my Ascot waistcoat—
Let's not risk it
Just to whisk it:
Yes, my Ascot waistcoat, Prescott.
Worn subfusc, it's
Cool and dusk: it
Might be grass-cut
But it's Ascot,
And it fits me like a gasket—
Ascot is *the* waistcoat, Prescott!
Please get
Off the spot of grease. Get
Going, Prescott—
Where's that waistcoat?
It's no task at
All, an Ascot:
Easy as to clean a musket
Or to dust an ivory tusk. It
Doesn't take a lot of fuss. Get
To it, Prescott,
Since I ask it:
We can't risk it—
Let's not whisk it.
That's the waistcoat;
Thank *you*, Prescott.

History of Education

The decent docent doesn't doze:
He teaches standing on his toes.
His student dassn't doze—and does,
And that's what teaching is and was.

Convalescence

I. The Nurses

The not-too-near slip softly by
Until I close a practice eye,
And then with instinct known as mother
They try to help me close the other.

II. The Fever Chart

Like Plimsoll lines on British hulls
My chart of temperature and pulse
Hangs from the bed, shows what I drink
And how much farther I can sink.

III. The Bed

My bed will fold up where I fold,
And arch its back, if all be told.
Providing angles as I choose,
My profiles run to "W's."

IV. The Visitors

The nurse looks round my clinic screen:
It's Mr. Jones or Mrs. Green.
Somehow my social self recurs;
I speak from strange interiors.

V. The Flowers

In slow recuperative hours
I cede the function of the flowers.
O keep them cold and crowd them in;
Reward them all with aspirin.

VI. The Letters

Letters are comforting to get.
Yes, I regret what they regret.
And I re-greet my dear regretters,
Livelier for Life & Letters.

VII. The Sneeze

I recommend for plain dis-ease
A good post-operandum sneeze;
You might as well be on the rack
When every stitch takes up its slack.

VIII. The Books

The books I have are made of lead—
They flatten me upon the bed.
A telegram is hard to hold:
Go easy on the Realms of Gold!

JOHN WHEELWRIGHT | 1897–1940

Week End Bid I

Where a fallen farmhouse leaves a scar	1
on the pasture, with a bed of pansies	2
with blackberries, black as caviar,	1
and Queen Anne's lace, and the coarser tansies	2
(grown in the century gone by	3
to keep away the dread swamp fevers)	4
with heights below me, and the height on high	3
of Quaker Hill of the True Believers,—	4
I plow the grasses, and tread the thistles	5
expectantly wondering where you are,	1
and that you send postcards for my epistles;	5
I turn, wherever a meadow bird whistles,	5
to catch you coming, and hear your cry.	3

Week End Bid II

I rise in the morning and close my shutter	1
to sleep, while the Sun swings from East to West;	2
and at night, when my lamps burn low and sputter,	1
put my head to bed to give it a rest.	2
Come here and talk to me. My muse and your muse	3
shall walk the pasture while we sleep,	4

that while we are waking, your views and my views 3
may grow more common-sense and deep 5
   (while distant milk trains clang to the city) 5
   in almost every word we utter 1
   and if not deeper, perhaps more witty. 5
   Come. If you don't, that will be a pity. 5
   Come if you can. You can, if you choose. 3

Lion

For William Lyon Phelps

One pucker lipping Lion's whelp (in flesh
called William Lyon Phelps) purrs: 'After all,—
there is no Opera like Lohengrin!
My father, a Baptist preacher, a good man
is now with God,—and every day is Christmas.
Apart from questions of creative genius,—
there are no gooder men than our good writers.
Lyman Abbott and I, who never could read Dante,
still found Cathedrals beautifully friendly.
Hell is OK; Purgatory bores me; Heaven's dull.
There is no Opera like Lohengrin!
Miss Lulu Bett's outline is a Greek statue.
Augustus Thomas' *Witching Hour*'s a masterpiece;
Housman's Second Volume is a masterpiece;
Anglo-Americans well know Oliphant's
masterpiece, *Bob, Son of Battle*, that masterpiece!
There is no Opera like Lohengrin!
In verse, these masterpieces are worth reading:

The Jar of Dreams by Lilla Cabot Perry;
Waves of Unrest by Bernice Lesbia Kenyon.'
(O Charlotte Endymion Porter! Percy Bysshe Shelley?
Helen Archibald Clark! O, women with three names!)
'Anna Hempstead Branch read all the Bible
through in a few days;—speaking of Milton,—
bad manners among critics are too common;
but gentlemen should not grow obsolete.
Often we fall asleep, not when we're bored,
but when we think we are most interesting.
There is no Opera like Lohengrin!
I sometimes think there are no persons who
can do more good than good librarians can.
American books grow easier to hold,—
dull paper and light weight is the Ideal.'

Marble-Top

At counters where I eat my lunch
   In dim arcades of industry,
I cock my elbows up and munch
   Whatever food occurs to me.

By many mirrors multiplied,
   My silly face is not exalted;
And when I leave I have inside
   An egg-and-lettuce and a malted.

And just to hear the pretty peal
   Of merry maids at their pimento
Is more to me than any meal
   Or banquet that I ever went to.

I Paint What I See

(A Ballad of Artistic Integrity, on the Occasion of the Removal of Some Rather Expensive Murals from the RCA Building in the Year 1933)

"What do you paint, when you paint on a wall?"
   Said John D.'s grandson Nelson.
"Do you paint just anything there at all?

"Will there be any doves, or a tree in fall?
"Or a hunting scene, like an English hall?"

"I paint what I see," said Rivera.

"What are the colors you use when you paint?"
    Said John D.'s grandson Nelson.
"Do you use any red in the beard of a saint?
"If you do, is it terribly red, or faint?
"Do you use any blue? Is it Prussian?"

"I paint what I paint," said Rivera.

"Whose is that head that I see on my wall?"
    Said John D.'s grandson Nelson.
"Is it anyone's head whom we know, at all?
"A Rensselaer, or a Saltonstall?
"Is it Franklin D.? Is it Mordaunt Hall?
"Or is it the head of a Russian?"

"I paint what I think," said Rivera.

"I paint what I paint, I paint what I see,
"I paint what I think," said Rivera,
"And the thing that is dearest in life to me
"In a bourgeois hall is Integrity;
"However . . .
"I'll take out a couple of people drinkin'
"And put in a picture of Abraham Lincoln;

"*I could even give you McCormick's reaper*
"*And still not make my art much cheaper.*
"*But the head of Lenin has got to stay*
"*Or my friend will give me the bird today,*
"*The bird, the bird, forever.*"

"It's not good taste in a man like me,"
    Said John D.'s grandson Nelson,

"To question an artist's integrity
"Or mention a practical thing like a fee,
"But I know what I like to a large degree,
    "Though art I hate to hamper;
"For twenty-one thousand conservative bucks
"You painted a radical. I say shucks,
    "I never could rent the offices—
    "The capitalistic offices.
"For this, as you know, is a public hall
"And people want doves, or a tree in fall,
"And though your art I dislike to hamper,
"I owe a *little* to God and Gramper,
    "And after all,
    "It's *my* wall . . ."

"*We'll see if it is,*" *said Rivera.*

Village Revisited

*(A cheerful lament in which truth, pain, and beauty are prominently
mentioned, and in that order)*

In the days of my youth, in the days of my youth,
I lay in West Twelfth Street, writhing with Truth.
I died in Jones Street, dallying with pain,
And flashed up Sixth Avenue, risen again.

In the terrible beautiful age of my prime,
I lacked for sweet linen but never for time.
The tree in the alley was potted in gold,
The girls on the buses would never grow old.

Last night with my love I returned to these haunts
To visit Pain's diggings and try for Truth's glance;
I was eager and ardent and waited as always
The answering click to my ring in the hallways,
But Truth hardly knew me, and Pain wasn't in
(It scarcely seemed possible Pain wasn't in).

Beauty recalled me. We bowed in the Square,
In the wonderful westerly Waverly air.
She had a new do, I observed, to her hair.

KENNETH FEARING | 1902–1961

Old Story

The drummer lad who marched away,
His uniform was bright with braid.
They may have wondered what he meant,
Or he himself wished he could say.
Doubtless he took his drum and played,
But what does it matter where he went,
And who cares whether he was gay,
Or whether he came back, or stayed?
His uniform was bright with braid,
His uniform was bright with braid.

Aphrodite Metropolis (III)

Harry loves Myrtle—He has strong arms from the
warehouse,
and on Sunday when they trolley to emerald meadows
he doesn't say
"What will your chastity amount to when your flesh
withers in a little while?"
No,
on Sunday when they trolley to emerald meadows
they look at the Sunday paper

"Girl Slays Banker-Betrayer"
they spread it around on the grass
"Bath-tub Stirs Jersey Row"
and then they sit down on it, nice.
Harry doesn't say "Ziggin's Ointment for withered flesh,
cures thousands of men and women of moles, warts, red
      veins,
flabby throat, scalp and hair diseases,
not expensive, and fully guaranteed."
No, Harry says nothing at all,
he smiles,
and they kiss in the emerald meadows on the Sunday
      paper.

Ballad of the Salvation Army

On Fourteenth street the bugles blow,
  Bugles blow, bugles blow.
The red, red, red, red banner floats
Where sweating angels split their throats,
Marching in burlap petticoats,
  Blow, bugles blow.

God is a ten car Bronx express,
  Red eyes round, red eyes round.
"Oh, where is my lustful lamb tonight,
His hair slicked down and his trousers tight?
I'll grind him back to my glory light!"
  Roll, subway, roll.

Heaven is a free amusement park,
   Big gold dome, big gold dome.
Movies at night: "The life she led."
Everyone sleeps in one big bed.
The stars go around inside your head.
   Home, sweet home.

Oh Fourteenth street the bugles blow,
   Bugles blow, bugles blow,
The torpid stones and pavements wake,
A million men and street-cars quake
In time with angel breasts that shake,
   Blow, bugles, blow!

Death and Transfiguration of Fourteenth Street

Fourteenth street, with a bad cold in its head,
Lay in a back bedroom on Fourteenth Street,
Not counting the rheumy flies that nailed the years
Speck upon speck to the walls overhead,
Not listening, dully, to the sleet, sleet, sleet
Of noise it had somehow sired by hoofs and gears
Drumming the xylophones of its deep stones,
Not knowing that Fourteenth Street would abruptly stop
When Murray opened his radio shop.

Tenderly over the corpse of Union Square
Murray's loud-speaker blats professional woe.
The malign, anemic whoop of Fourteenth Street

Chokes sickly on the opera-tainted air,
Laocoon to the hugely brooding flow
Of stuffed serpents, too glistening, and sweet.
The toil of many flies is snow-capped, and done.
The angels weep while Murray, in the mist,
Paddles the pants of Fourteenth Street with Liszt.

Cultural Notes

Professor Burke's symphony "Colorado Vistas"
In four movements,
  I   Mountains
  II Canyons
 III Dusk
 IV Dawn
Was played recently by the Philharmonic.
Snap-shots of the localities described in music were
    passed around.
The audience checked for accuracy.
All O.K.
After the performance Maurice Epstein, twenty-nine,
    tuberculosis,
Stoker on the S.S. Tarboy,
Rose to his feet and shouted:
"He's crazy! Them artists are all crazy,
I can prove it by Max Nordau,
They poison the minds of young girls."
Otto Svoboda, 500 Avenue A, butcher, Pole, husband,
    philosopher,

Argued in rebuttal: "Shut your trap, you!
The question is, does the symphony fit in with Karl
    Marx?"
At the Friday evening meeting of the Browning Writing
    League
Mrs. Whittamore Ralston-Beckett, traveler, lecturer,
    novelist, critic, poet, playwright, editor, mother,
    idealist,
Fascinated her audience in a brief talk, whimsical and
    caustic
Appealing to the younger generation to take a brighter,
    happier, more sunny and less morbid
View of life's unchanging fundamentals.
Mrs. Ralston-Beckett quoted Sir Horace Bennet. "O
    Beauty," she said,
"Take your fingers off my throat, take your elbow out of
    my eye,
Take your sorrow off my sorrow,
Take your hat, take your gloves, take your feet down off
    the table,
Take your beauty off my beauty, and go."
After the performance Maurice Epstein, twenty-nine,
    tuberculosis,
Stoker on the S.S. Tarboy,
Kicked to his feet and screamed:
"She's crazy! Them artists are all crazy!
I can prove it by Max Nordau
They poison the minds of young girls."
Otto Svoboda, butcher, Pole, husband, philosopher,
Spoke in reply: "Shut your trap, you!
The question is, what about Karl Marx?"

Dirge

1–2–3 was the number he played but today the number
      came 3–2–1;
  bought his Carbide at 30 and it went to 29; had the
      favorite at Bowie but the track was slow—

O, executive type, would you like to drive a floating
      power, knee-action, silk-upholstered six? Wed a
      Hollywood star? Shoot the course in 58? Draw
      to the ace, king, jack?
  O, fellow with a will who won't take no, watch out for
      three cigarettes on the same, single match; O,
      democratic voter born in August under Mars,
      beware of liquidated rails—

Denouement to denouement, he took a personal pride
      in the certain, certain way he lived his own,
      private life,
  but nevertheless, they shut off his gas; nevertheless, the
      bank foreclosed; nevertheless, the landlord
      called; nevertheless, the radio broke,

And twelve o'clock arrived just once too often,
  just the same he wore one grey tweed suit, bought
      one straw hat, drank one straight Scotch, walked
      one short step, took one long look, drew one
      deep breath,
  just one too many,

And wow he died as wow he lived,
    going whop to the office and blooie home to sleep
        and biff got married and bam had children and
        oof got fired,
    zowie did he live and zowie did he die,

With who the hell are you at the corner of his casket,
        and where the hell we going on the right-hand
        silver knob, and who the hell cares walking
        second from the end with an American Beauty
        wreath from why the hell not,

Very much missed by the circulation staff of the New
        York Evening Post; deeply, deeply mourned by
        the B.M.T.,

Wham, Mr. Roosevelt; pow, Sears Roebuck; awk, big
        dipper; bop, summer rain;
    bong, Mr., bong, Mr., bong, Mr., bong.

OGDEN NASH | 1902–1971

Spring Comes to Murray Hill

I sit in an office at 244 Madison Avenue,
And say to myself you have a responsible job, havenue?
Why then do you fritter away your time on this
    doggerel?
If you have a sore throat you can cure it by using a good
    goggeral,
If you have a sore foot you can get it fixed by a
    chiropodist
And you can get your original sin removed by St. John
    the Bopodist,
Why then should this flocculent lassitude be incurable?
Kansas City, Kansas, proves that even Kansas City
    needn't always be Missourible.
Up up my soul! This inaction is abdominable.
The pilgrims settled Massachusetts in 1620 when they
    landed on a stone hummock.
Maybe if they were here now they would settle my
    stomach.
Oh, if I only had the wings of a bird
Instead of being confined on Madison Avenue I could
    soar in a jiffy to Second or Third.

Watchman, What of the First First Lady?

Everybody can tell you the date of George Washington's
     birth,
But who knows the date on which Mrs. George
     Washington first appeared on earth?
Isn't there any justice
For the former Mrs. Custis?
Of course her memory is perpetuated by a hotel,
But Hell.
It's a disgrace to every United State
That we don't know more about our first president's
     only mate.
We all know a lot of stories about the wife of King Arthur
But you never hear any about Martha,
And we have all read a lot of romantic tales about
     Napoleon's Empress's life
But nobody even writes them about Washington's wife,
And we have all seen Katharine Cornell or Helen Hayes
     or Ethel Barrymore
Impersonate Cleopatra, who wasn't even anybody's real
     wife but nothing more or less than a promiscuous
     un-American parrymore,
And watched George Bernard Shaw with the skill of a
     surgeon
Dissect Joan of Arc, who was neither a wife nor a
     paramour but nothing but a vurgeon.
But has anybody done anything about the mistress of
     the nation's whitest house?
No, and yet but for her the nation would be the child of
     a man without a spouse.

Please Pass the Biscuit

I have a little dog,
Her name is Spangle.
And when she eats
I think she'll strangle.

She's darker than Hamlet,
Lighter than Porgy;
Her heart is gold,
Her odor, dorgy.

Her claws click-click
Across the floor,
Her nose is always
Against a door.

The squirrel flies
Her pursuing mouth;
Should he fly north,
She pursues him south.

Yet do not mock her
As she hunts;
Remember, she caught
A milkman once.

Like liquid gems
Her eyes burn clearly;
She's five years old,
And house-trained, nearly.

Her shame is deep
When she has erred;
She dreads the blow
Less than the word.

I marvel that such
Small ribs as these
Can cage such vast
Desire to please.

She's as much a part
Of the house as the mortgage;
Spangle, I wish you
A ripe old dortgage.

The Termite

Some primal termite knocked on wood
And tasted it, and found it good,
And that is why your Cousin May
Fell through the parlor floor today.

The Panther

The panther is like a leopard,
Except it hasn't been peppered.
Should you behold a panther crouch,
Prepare to say Ouch.
Better yet, if called by a panther,
Don't anther.

A Beginner's Guide to the Ocean

Let us now consider the ocean.
It is always in motion.
It is generally understood to be the source of much of
    our rain,
And ten thousand fleets are said to have swept over it in
    vain.
When the poet requested it to break break break on its
    cold gray rocks it obligingly broke broke broke.
Which as the poet was Alfred Lord Tennyson didn't
    surprise him at all but if it had been me I would
    probably have had a stroke.
Some people call it the Atlantic and some the Pacific or
    the Antarctic or the Indian or the Mediterranean
    Sea,
But I always say what difference does it make, some old
    geographer mumbling a few words of it, it will
    always be just the Ocean to me.

There is an immortal dignity about something like the
    Atlantic,
Which seems to drive unimmortal undignified human
    beings frustratedly frantic.
Just give them one foot on the beach and people who
    were perfectly normal formerly, or whilom,
Why, they are subject to whoops and capers that would
    get them blackballed from an asylum;
Yet be they never so rampant and hollerant,
The ocean is tolerant,
Except a couple of times a day it gives up in disgust and
    goes off by itself and hides,
And that, my dears, accounts for the tides.

Kind of an Ode to Duty

O Duty,
Why has thou not the visage of a sweetie or a cutie?
Why displayest thou the countenance of the kind of
    conscientious organizing spinster
That the minute you see her you are aginster?
Why glitter thy spectacles so ominously?
Why art thou clad so abominously?
Why art thou so different from Venus
And why do thou and I have so few interests mutually in
    common between us?
Why art thou fifty per cent martyr
And fifty-one per cent Tartar?
Why is it thy unfortunate wont

To try to attract people by calling on them either to
leave undone the deeds they like, or to do the deeds
they don't?
Why art thou so like an April post mortem
On something that died in the autumn?
Above all, why dost thou continue to hound me?
Why art thou always albatrossly hanging around me?
Thou so ubiquitous,
And I so iniquitous.
I seem to be the one person in the world thou art
perpetually preaching at who or to who;
Whatever looks like fun, there art thou standing
between me and it, calling yoo-hoo.
O Duty, Duty!
How noble a man should I be hadst thou the visage of a
sweetie or a cutie!
Wert thou but houri instead of hag
Then would my halo indeed be in the bag!
But as it is thou art so much forbiddinger than a
Wodehouse hero's forbiddingest aunt
That in the words of the poet, When Duty whispers
low, Thou must, this erstwhile youth replies, I just
can't.

No Wonder Our Fathers Died

Does anybody mind if I don't live in a house that is
quaint?
Because, for one thing, quaint houses are generally
houses where plumbing ain't,

And while I don't hold with fanatical steel-and-glass
modernistic bigots,
Still, I do think that it simplifies life if you live it
surrounded by efficient pipes and faucets and
spiggots.
I admit that wells and pumps and old oaken buckets are
very nice in a poem or ode,
But I feel that in literature is where they should have
their permanent abode,
Because suppose you want a bath,
It is pleasanter to be able to take it without leaving a
comfortable stuffy room and going out into the
bracing fresh air and bringing back some water
from the end of a path.
Another thing about which I am very earnest,
Is that I do like a house to be properly furnaced,
Because if I am out in the bracing fresh air I expect to
be frozen,
But to be frigid in a stuffy room isn't what I would have
chosen.
And when you go to bed in a quaint house the whole
house grumbles and mutters,
And you are sure the walls will be shattered by clattering
shutters.
At least you hope it's the shutters but you fear it's a gang
of quaint ghosts warming up for twelve o'clock,
And you would lock yourself snugly in but the quaint
old key won't turn in the quaint old lock,
So you would pull the bedclothes snugly up over your
head and lie there till a year from next autumn,

Were it not a peculiarity of bedclothes in quaint houses
that if you pull them up on top, why your feet stick
out at the bautum,
But anyhow you find a valley among the hilltops of your
mattress and after a while slumber comes softly
stealing,
And that is when you feel a kiss on your cheek and you
think maybe it is a goodnight kiss from your
guardian angel, but it isn't, it's a leak in the ceiling.
Oh, I yield to none in my admiration of the hardy
colonists and their hardy spouses,
But I still feel that their decadent descendants build
more comfortable houses.

A Necessary Dirge

Sometimes it's difficult, isn't it, not to grow grim and
rancorous
Because man's fate is so counter-clockwise and
cantankerous.
Look at all the noble projects that die a-borning,
Look how hard it is to get to sleep at night and then
how hard it is to wake up in the morning!
How easy to be unselfish in the big things that never
come up and how hard in the little things that
come up daily and hourly, oh yes,
Such as what heroic pleasure to give up the last seat in a
lifeboat to a mother and babe, and what an
irritation to give some housewife your seat on the
Lexington Avenue Express!

How easy for those who do not bulge
To not overindulge!
O universe perverse, why and whence your perverseness?
Why do you not teem with betterness instead of worseness?
Do you get your only enjoyment
Out of humanity's annoyment?
Because a point I would like to discuss
Is, why wouldn't it be just as easy for you to make things
　　easy for us?
But no, you will not listen, expostulation is useless,
Home is the fisherman empty-handed, home is the
　　hunter caribouless and mooseless.
Humanity must continue to follow the sun around
And accept the eternal run-around.
Well, and if that be the case, why come on humanity!
So long as it is our fate to be irked all our life let us just
　　keep our heads up and take our irking with
　　insouciant urbanity.

The Private Dining Room

Miss Rafferty wore taffeta,
Miss Cavendish wore lavender.
We ate pickerel and mackerel
And other lavish provender.
Miss Cavendish was Lalage,
Miss Rafferty was Barbara.
We gobbled pickled mackerel
And broke the candelabara,

Miss Cavendish in lavender,
In taffeta, Miss Rafferty,
The girls in taffeta lavender,
And we, of course, in mufti.

Miss Rafferty wore taffeta,
The taffeta was lavender,
Was lavend, lavender, lavenderest,
As the wine improved the provender.
Miss Cavendish wore lavender,
The lavender was taffeta.
We boggled mackled pickerel,
And bumpers did we quaffeta.
And Lalage wore lavender,
And lavender wore Barbara,
Rafferta taffeta Cavender lavender
Barbara abracadabra.

Miss Rafferty in taffeta
Grew definitely raffisher.
Miss Cavendish in lavender
Grew less and less stand-offisher.
With Lalage and Barbara
We grew a little pickereled,
We ordered Mumm and Roederer
Because the bubbles tickereled.
But lavender and taffeta
Were gone when we were soberer.
I haven't thought for thirty years
Of Lalage and Barbara.

What's In a Name? Some Letter I Always Forget

Not only can I not remember anecdotes that are racy,
But I also can't remember whether the names of my
    Scottish friends begin with M-c or M-a-c,
And I can't speak for you, but for myself there is one
    dilemma with me in the middle of it,
Which is, is it Katharine with a K or Catherine with a
    C, and furthermore is it an A or is it an E in the
    middle of it?
I can remember the races between Man o' War and Sir
    Barton, and Épinard and Zev,
But I can't remember whether it's Johnson or Johnston
    any more than whether you address a minister as
    Mr. or Dr. or simply Rev.
I know a cygnet from a gosling and a coney from a leveret,
But how to distinguish an I-double-T from an E-double-T
    Everett?
I am familiar with the nature of an oath,
But I get confused between the Eliot with one L and
    one T, and the Elliot with two L's and one T, and
    the Eliott with one L and two T's, and the Elliott
    with two of both.
How many of my friendships have lapsed because of an
    extra T or a missing L;
Give me a simple name like Taliaferro or Wambsganss
    or Toporcer or Joralemon or Mankiewicz that any
    schoolboy can spell,
Because many former friends thought I was being
    impolite to them

When it was only because I couldn't remember whether
     they were Stuarts with a U or Stewarts with an
     E-W that I didn't write to them.

Arthur

There was an old man of Calcutta,
Who coated his tonsils with butta,
Thus converting his snore
From a thunderous roar
To a soft, oleaginous mutta.

The Song of Songs

Is anybody here in favor of a redistribution of wealth?
Because I think it ought to be redistributed, only not by
     force or by stealth,
Because it is only when other people have it and you
     haven't that it is evil,
So we had better try to correct the situation before it is
     made worse by a revolution or an upheaval.
Let us not be like the Soviets and fall prey to any
     communistic demagog,
No, surely we have more sense than a mujik and would
     yawn at arguments that keep them agog;
And let us not be sheep like a Fascist audience

Who get played on by their leaders like concertinas or
    accaudience;
Let us rather correct in our own 100% American way
    the wrongs that annoy and disgust us,
And correct them so the corrections will not offend the
    Constitution and Mr. Hughes, our imposing Chief
    Justice;
Let us handle it in the manner of Washington and
    Jefferson and Jackson
And keep very level-headed and Anglo-Saxon.
There are several things standing in the way of a natural
    distribution of wealth, but if you want to know
    which is the chief thing, well, I will tell you which:
The rich marry only the rich.
It is one of our national disasters
That, broadly speaking, Astors and Vanderbilts and
    Rockefellers and Morgans never marry anybody
    but Morgans and Rockefellers and Vanderbilts and
    Astors,
Whereas if they only bestowed their affections on some-
    body in a lower crust,
Why money would be distributed over this broad land
    of ours like dust,
So I think they may all be rich but honest,
But I think their matchmaking proclivities ought to be
    harnessed.
Yes, if money marrying money were prohibited,
How speedily and how painlessly it would be
    redistributed.
Yes, yes, the rich and the poor can settle and forget their
    differences just as the Blue and the Gray have

As soon as we have a law saying that people can only
　　　marry people who have a lot less money than they
　　　have,
And that will be the end of all your present and future
　　　Townsends and Coughlins and Longs,
And that is why I call this piece the Song of Songs.

View from a Suburban Window

When I consider how my light is spent,
     Also my sweetness, ditto all my power,
Papering shelves or saving for the rent
     Or prodding grapefruit while the grocers glower,
Or dulcetly persuading to the dentist
     The wailing young, or fitting them for shoes,
Beset by menus and my days apprenticed
     Forever to a grinning household muse;

And how I might, in some tall town instead,
     From nine to five be furthering a Career,
     Dwelling unfettered in my single flat,
My life my own, likewise my daily bread—
     When I consider this, it's very clear
     I might have done much worse. I might, at that.

Trinity Place

The pigeons that peck at the grass in Trinity Churchyard
     Are pompous as bankers. They walk with an air, they
          preen
Their prosperous feathers. They smugly regard their
          beauty.

They are plump, they are sleek. It is only the men who
    are lean.
The pigeons scan with disfavor the men who sit there,
    Listless in sun or shade. The pigeons sidle
Between the gravestones with shrewd, industrious
    motions.
    The pigeons are busy. It is only the men who are idle.
The pigeons sharpen their beaks on the stones, and they
    waddle
    In dignified search of their proper, their daily bread.
Their eyes are small with contempt for the men on the
    benches.
    It is only the men who are hungry. The pigeons are fed.

Why, Some of My Best Friends Are Women

I learned in my credulous youth
    That women are shallow as fountains.
Women make lies out of truth
    And out of a molehill their mountains.
Women are giddy and vain,
    Cold-hearted or tiresomely tender;
Yet, nevertheless, I maintain
    I dote on the feminine gender.

For the female of the species may be deadlier than the male
But she can make herself a cup of coffee without reducing
The entire kitchen to a shambles.

Perverse though their taste in cravats
    Is deemed by their lords and their betters,
They know the importance of hats
    And they write you the news in their letters.
Their minds may be lighter than foam,
    Or altered in haste and in hurry,
But they seldom bring company home
    When you're warming up yesterday's curry.

And when lovely woman stoops to folly,
She does not invariably come in at four A.M.
Singing "Sweet Adeline."

Oh, women are frail and they weep.
    They are recklessly given to scions.
But, wakened unduly from sleep,
    They are milder than tigers or lions.
Women hang clothes on their pegs
    Nor groan at the toil and the trouble.
Women have rather nice legs
    And chins that are guiltless of stubble.
Women are restless, uneasy to handle,
But when they are burning both ends of the scandal,
They do not insist with a vow that is votive,
How high are their minds and how noble the motive.

As shopping companions they're heroes and saints;
They meet you in tearooms nor murmur complaints;
They listen, entranced, to a list of your vapors;
At breakfast they sometimes emerge from the papers;

A Brave Little Widow's not apt to sob-story 'em,
And they keep a cool head in a grocery emporium.
Yes, I rise to defend
   The quite possible She.
For the feminine gend-
   Er is O.K. by me.

Besides, everybody admits it's a Man's World.
And just look what they've done to it!

Evening Musicale

Candles. Red tulips, ninety cents the bunch.
   Two lions, Grade B. A newly tuned piano.
No cocktails, but a dubious kind of punch,
   Lukewarm and weak. A harp and a soprano.
The "Lullaby" of Brahms. Somebody's cousin
   From Forest Hills, addicted to the pun.
Two dozen gentlemen; ladies, three dozen,
   Earringed and powdered. Sandwiches at one.

The ash trays few, the ventilation meager.
   Shushes to greet the late-arriving guest
Or quell the punch-bowl group. A young man eager
   To render "Danny Deever" by request.
And sixty people trying to relax
On little rented chairs with gilded backs.

Blues for a Melodeon

A castor's loose on the buttoned chair—
   The one upholstered in shabby coral.
I never noticed, before, that tear
   In the dining-room paper.

When did the rocker cease to rock,
   The fringe sag down on the corner sofa?
All of a sudden the Meissen clock
   Has a cherub missing.

All of a sudden the plaster chips,
   The carpet frays by the morning windows;
Careless, a rod from the curtain slips,
   And the gilt is tarnished.

This is the house that I knew by heart.
   Everything here seemed sound, immortal.
When did this delicate ruin start?
   How did the moth come?

Naked by daylight, the paint is airing
   Its rags and tatters. There's dust on the mantel.
And who is that gray-haired stranger staring
   Out of my mirror?

New England Pilgrimage

THE CUSTOMS OF THE COUNTRY

Connecticut, with much at stake,
Prefers to call a pool a lake,
But in New Hampshire and beyond
They like to call a lake a pond.

LANDSCAPE WITH FIGURINES

Vermont has mountains,
Vermont has pines,
Has highways innocent of billboard signs,
Has white front porches, neighborly and wandering,
Where ladies hang the laundry
When they feel like laundering.

People in Vermont
Keep their tongues well-throttled,
Have carbonated summertimes that should be bottled,
Have cows like goddesses and cats like pandas.
But they *will* hang their washing
On their front verandas.

HAPPY TIME

It goes to the heart,
It goes to the head
To look on lobster
When it's red.
Lobster, native on a *carte du jour*, may
Make a gourmand out of a gourmet.

Theater-in-the-Barn

Old Guernsey ghosts—do they recall, with shock,
When they were the sole stars of summer stock?

Memo for Duncan Hines

Russians are fond of caviar.
    The French, whom nothing ruffles,
Admire the pale
Reclusive snail,
    And send their pigs for truffles.
The Swedes hold court
With smorgasbord.
    But down New England way,
Where once the bean
Was high cuisine,
    Behold the Relish Tray!

> *Don't look now,*
> *But here it comes:*
> *Cinnamon apples,*
> *Candied plums,*
> *Fanciful notions*
> *Like pickled peas,*
> *And oceans and oceans*
> *Of cottage cheese.*

I've ordered oysters on the Cape
    When empty was the bucket.
The chowder bowl
That soothes the soul
    Has failed me in Nantucket.

I've found Vermont
At times in want
　　Of turkey, which was hellish.
But who has been
At any Inn
　　Immaculate of Relish?

　　　　Dine at Danbury,
　　　　Lunch at Noone.
　　　　A similar cranberry
　　　　Stains the spoon.
　　　　It's onions at Dover
　　　　To spice the breeze,
　　　　And over and over
　　　　It's cottage cheese.

There's many a gastronomic gulf
　　No alien palate bridges.
On Britain's coast
They toast their toast,
　　Then cool it in their fridges.
Chinese say grace
Above a brace
　　Of birds' nest rolled in batter.
But, Haddam Neck
To the Kennebec,
　　There reigns the Relish Platter.

Butter your muffin,
Order your filet,
Harbor your strength
For the piccalilli,
For things in an umber
Mustard mix,
The sweet cucumber,
The carrot sticks,
The celery twisted
Like tropic trees,
And the cottage cheese.
And the cottage cheese.

AFTERNOON TEA AT THE COLONY

In Peterboro or on its margin
  (Where I was visiting at),
I watched the authors roaming at large in
  Their natural habitat.
Tranced, on the slopes of the Great McDow'll,
I saw them feed, I heard them growl.
But try as I would, I couldn't tell
Which was lion
And which gazelle.

SIC TRANSIT

Although these days it makes my hair lift—
Descending Mansfield in a chair lift—
Now (over twenty-one and freeborn)
I'd rather ride down than be ski-borne.

Concerning Maine Swimming

Glacial and glittery,
The waters off Kittery.
I dread to dunk
At Kennebunk.
But that cool wave
Past Bath and Bristol
I wouldn't brave
At the point of a pistol.

The Day After Sunday

Always on Monday, God's in the morning papers,
    His Name is a headline, His Works are rumored abroad.
Having been praised by men who are movers and shapers,
    From prominent Sunday pulpits, newsworthy is God.

On page 27, just opposite Fashion Trends,
    One reads at a glance how He scolded the Baptists a
        little,
Was firm with the Catholics, practical with the Friends,
    To Unitarians pleasantly noncommittal.

In print are His numerous aspects, too: God smiling,
    God vexed, God thunderous, God whose mansions
        are pearl,
Political God, God frugal, God reconciling
    Himself with science, God guiding the Camp Fire Girl.

Always on Monday morning the press reports
    God as revealed to His vicars in various guises—
Benevolent, stormy, patient, or out of sorts.
    God knows which God is the God God recognizes.

HELEN BEVINGTON | 1906–2001

Mr. Rockefeller's Hat

The time I went to church I sat
By Mr. Rockefeller's hat.
It stood upon its silken crown,
A lovely sheen along the brim,
Distracting, even upside down,
Disturbing every prayer and hymn,
With three initials in pure gold
Aglitter from the lining's fold.

Beside me on the crimson plush,
It shimmered gravely in the hush
Of potted calla lilies, ferns,
Of stately tapers decorously
Alight, of gracious blooms in urns,
All odorous of sanctity.
It added lustre to the view
Of Mr. Rockefeller, too.

To Helen

Helen, thy beauty is to me
A beautiful anomaly.
Ten thousand ships depart a place
With no persuasion from my face.
Ten thousand ships would rot in port
With my face still their last resort.
A name both pagan and divine
Is Helen, classical and mine,
If I was not meant to embarrass
By plethora of riches, Paris.

The Princess and the Pea

The Princess slept uneasily
Upon a small, offending pea

And twenty mattresses that were
Between the vegetable and her.

Her royal person, rather plump,
Was agitated by a lump

That we, more hardy, would have said
Was never bothersome in bed.

Some people mind, and she was one.
The simple moral is, my son,

Avoid a Princess, shun a palace,
And pick a wife more lean and callous.

Ballade of Poetic Material

Poets sing of a love forlorn
(Love denied and a heart that breaks),
A popular wail since Eve was born,
From Sappho's isle to the English Lakes.
But give them credit for what it takes
To scour the mind and sweep the brain.
Here is a theme: (now two it makes)
Poets sing of the wind and rain.

Sure as the dawn tomorrow morn,
Old as the taste of ducks for drakes,
Each is a matter tried and worn
As lust in Restoration rakes.
But where's the harm if the Muse awakes
To barometer and weathervane,
Love grows damper than water snakes,
Poets sing of the wind and rain?

Critics may scoff and point with scorn,
Mencken prattle of belly-aches.
(What should we have them do, adorn
Their lines with recipes for cakes?)
Stand the Anointed for whose sakes
Love and Wonder and Light remain,
Love and Beauty and white snowflakes,
Poets sing of the wind and rain.

Prince, we live in a world of fakes,
Lies and leers and legerdemain.
God be thanked while the planet shakes
Poets sing of the wind and rain.

W. H. AUDEN | 1907–1973

Under Which Lyre
A Reactionary Tract for the Times
(Phi Beta Kappa Poem, Harvard, 1946)

Ares at last has quit the field,
The bloodstains on the bushes yield
   To seeping showers,
And in their convalescent state
The fractured towns associate
   With summer flowers.

Encamped upon the college plain
Raw veterans already train
   As freshman forces;
Instructors with sarcastic tongue
Shepherd the battle-weary young
   Through basic courses.

Among bewildering appliances
For mastering the arts and sciences
   They stroll or run,
And nerves that steeled themselves to slaughter
Are shot to pieces by the shorter
   Poems of Donne.

Professors back from secret missions
Resume their proper eruditions,
    Though some regret it;
They liked their dictaphones a lot,
They met some big wheels, and do not
    Let you forget it.

But Zeus' inscrutable decree
Permits the will-to-disagree
    To be pandemic,
Ordains that vaudeville shall preach
And every commencement speech
    Be a polemic.

Let Ares doze, that other war
Is instantly declared once more
    'Twixt those who follow
Precocious Hermes all the way
And those who without qualms obey
    Pompous Apollo.

Brutal like all Olympic games,
Though fought with smiles and Christian names
    And less dramatic,
This dialectic strife between
The civil gods is just as mean,
    And more fanatic.

What high immortals do in mirth
Is life and death on Middle Earth;
    Their a-historic

Antipathy forever gripes
All ages and somatic types,
   The sophomoric

Who face the future's darkest hints
With giggles or with prairie squints
   As stout as Cortez,
And those who like myself turn pale
As we approach with ragged sail
   The fattening forties.

The sons of Hermes love to play,
And only do their best when they
   Are told they oughtn't;
Apollo's children never shrink
From boring jobs but have to think
   Their work important.

Related by antithesis,
A compromise between us is
   Impossible;
Respect perhaps but friendship never:
Falstaff the fool confronts forever
   The prig Prince Hal.

If he would leave the self alone,
Apollo's welcome to the throne,
   Fasces and falcons;
He loves to rule, has always done it;
The earth would soon, did Hermes run it,
   Be like the Balkans.

But jealous of our god of dreams,
His common-sense in secret schemes
   To rule the heart;
Unable to invent the lyre,
Creates with simulated fire
   Official art.

And when he occupies a college,
Truth is replaced by Useful Knowledge;
   He pays particular
Attention to Commercial Thought,
Public Relations, Hygiene, Sport,
   In his curricula.

Athletic, extrovert and crude,
For him, to work in solitude
   Is the offence,
The goal a populous Nirvana:
His shield bears this device: *Mens sana
   Qui mal y pense.*

Today his arms, we must confess,
From Right to Left have met success,
   His banners wave
From Yale to Princeton, and the news
From Broadway to the Book Reviews
   Is very grave.

His radio Homers all day long
In over-Whitmanated song
   That does not scan,

With adjectives laid end to end,
Extol the doughnut and commend
   The Common Man.

His, too, each homely lyric thing
On sport or spousal love or spring
   Or dogs or dusters,
Invented by some court-house bard
For recitation by the yard
   In filibusters.

To him ascend the prize orations
And sets of fugal variations
   On some folk-ballad,
While dietitians sacrifice
A glass of prune-juice or a nice
   Marsh-mallow salad.

Charged with his compound of sensational
Sex plus some undenominational
   Religious matter,
Enormous novels by co-eds
Rain down on our defenceless heads
   Till our teeth chatter.

In fake Hermetic uniforms
Behind our battle-line, in swarms
   That keep alighting,
His existentialists declare
That they are in complete despair,
   Yet go on writing.

No matter; He shall be defied;
White Aphrodite is on our side:
    What though his threat
To organize us grow more critical?
Zeus willing, we, the unpolitical,
    Shall beat him yet.

Lone scholars, sniping from the walls
Of learned periodicals,
    Our facts defend,
Our intellectual marines,
Landing in little magazines,
    Capture a trend.

By night our student Underground
At cocktail parties whisper round
    From ear to ear;
Fat figures in the public eye
Collapse next morning, ambushed by
    Some witty sneer.

In our morale must lie our strength:
So, that we may behold at length
    Routed Apollo's
Battalions melt away like fog,
Keep well the Hermetic Decalogue,
    Which runs as follows:—

Thou shalt not do as the dean pleases.
Thou shalt not write thy doctor's thesis
    On education,

Thou shalt not worship projects nor
Shalt thou or thine bow down before
    Administration.

Thou shalt not answer questionnaires
Or quizzes upon World-Affairs,
    Nor with compliance
Take any test. Thou shalt not sit
With statisticians nor commit
    A social science.

Thou shalt not be on friendly terms
With guys in advertising firms,
    Nor speak with such
As read the Bible for its prose,
Nor, above all, make love to those
    Who wash too much.

Thou shalt not live within thy means
Nor on plain water and raw greens.
    If thou must choose
Between the chances, choose the odd:
Read *The New Yorker*, trust in God;
    And take short views.

(In Memoriam Ogden Nash)

My First Name, Wystan,
Rhymes with Tristan,
But—O dear!—I do hope
I'm not quite such a dope.

——

John Milton
Never stayed in a Hilton
Hotel,
Which was just as well.

——

Oscar Wilde
Was greatly beguiled,
When into the Café Royal walked Bosie
Wearing a tea-cosy.

Parable

The watch upon my wrist
Would soon forget that I exist,
If it were not reminded
By days when I forget to wind it.

FROM **Uncoupled Couplets**

WILLIAM SHAKESPEARE
When my love swears that she is made of truth,
All I can do is blame it on her youth.

ROBERT HERRICK
Whenas in silks my Julia goes,
The outline of her girdle shows.

ROBERT HERRICK
Gather ye Rosebuds while ye may
But take your little pill each day.

THOMAS CAMPION
There is a garden in her face;
Her dermatologist has the case.

ALGERNON CHARLES SWINBURNE
When the hounds of spring are on winter's traces,
The rich take off for warmer places.

ANTHONY HECHT | b. 1923

The Dover Bitch
A Criticism of Life

for Andrews Wanning

So there stood Matthew Arnold and this girl
With the cliffs of England crumbling away behind them,
And he said to her, "Try to be true to me,
And I'll do the same for you, for things are bad
All over, etc., etc."
Well now, I knew this girl. It's true she had read
Sophocles in a fairly good translation
And caught that bitter allusion to the sea,
But all the time he was talking she had in mind
The notion of what his whiskers would feel like
On the back of her neck. She told me later on
That after a while she got to looking out
At the lights across the channel, and really felt sad,
Thinking of all the wine and enormous beds
And blandishments in French and the perfumes.
And then she got really angry. To have been brought
All the way down from London, and then be addressed
As a sort of mournful cosmic last resort
Is really tough on a girl, and she was pretty.
Anyway, she watched him pace the room
And finger his watch-chain and seem to sweat a bit,
And then she said one or two unprintable things.

But you mustn't judge her by that. What I mean to say is,
She's really all right. I still see her once in a while
And she always treats me right. We have a drink
And I give her a good time, and perhaps it's a year
Before I see her again, but there she is,
Running to fat, but dependable as they come.
And sometimes I bring her a bottle of *Nuit d'Amour*.

Handicap

Higgledy-piggledy
Judas Iscariot,
Cloven of palate, of
Voice insecure,

Mumbler and lisper, was
Hypocoristically
Known to his buddies as
"Jude, the Obscure."

It Never Rains . . .

Patty-cake, patty-cake,
Jupiter Pluvius,
Antediluvian
Rain-making chap,

Showered his masculine
Potentialities
All over Danae's
Succulent lap.

Firmness

Higgledy-piggledy
Mme. de Maintenon*
Shouted, "Up yours!" when ap-
Proached for the rent,

And, in her anger, pro-
Ceeded to demonstrate,
Iconographically,
Just what she meant.

* "On the King's death she retired altogether to St. Cyr. It is surprising
that the king left her almost nothing; he simply recommended her to
the care of the Duke of Orleans."

VOLTAIRE, *The Age of Louis XIV*

From the Grove Press

Higgledy-piggledy
Ralph Waldo Emerson
Wroth at Bostonian,
Cowardly hints,

Wrote an unprintable
Epithalamion
Based on a volume of
Japanese prints.

Down There on a Visit

Higgledy-piggledy
Gustav von Aschenbach,
Fed to the gullet with
High German joys,

Sought in an atmosphere
Mediterranean
Soft, antinomian
Decadent boys.

EDWARD GOREY | 1925–2000

From the bathing machine came a din
As of jollification within;
   It was heard far and wide,
   And the incoming tide
Had a definite flavour of gin.

———

The *Proctor* buys a pupil ices,
   And hopes the boy will not resist
When he attempts to practise vices
   Few people even know exist.

Variations on a Theme by William Carlos Williams

1

I chopped down the house that you had been saving to
    live in next summer.
I am sorry, but it was morning, and I had nothing to do
and its wooden beams were so inviting.

2

We laughed at the hollyhocks together
and then I sprayed them with lye.
Forgive me. I simply do not know what I am doing.

3

I gave away the money that you had been saving to live
    on for the next ten years.
The man who asked for it was shabby
and the firm March wind on the porch was so juicy and
    cold.

4

Last evening we went dancing and I broke your leg.
Forgive me. I was clumsy, and
I wanted you here in the wards, where I am the doctor!

La Ville de Nice

O harbor for the rich and poor
O plain yet evanescent
O married man and paramour
O peacock born of pheasant

The first time that I walked through your
Streets, still to the earth a present,
Twenty years old, on tour,
Once near my ear a husky pleasant

Voice intoned "Est-ce que tu
Ne voudrais pas la joie?"
Not knowing what to do,
I went to my hotel, l'Hôtel du Roi

Saying that surprising word (la joie)
And kept on saying it until
I'd gone from Nice to Cannes
And then kept traveling on.

Above All That?

Higgledy-piggledy
Mary of Magdala
Said to the dolorous
Mother of God:

"Parthenogenesis
I for one left to the
Simple amoeba or
Gasteropod."

Neo-Classic

Higgledy-piggledy
Jacqueline Kennedy
Went back to Hydra and
Found it a mess—

Neon lights, discotheques . . .
"Landlord, what's *hap*pening?"
"'Ανθρωπιστήκαμε*
Go home, U.S."

* or, roughly, "We have become human beings!"

Tomorrows

The question was an academic one.
Andrey Sergeyvitch, rising sharp at two,
Would finally write that letter to his three
Sisters still in the country. Stop at four,
Drink tea, dress elegantly and, by five,
Be losing money at the Club des Six.

In Pakistan a band of outraged Sikhs
Would storm an embassy (the wrong one)
And spend the next week cooling off in five
Adjacent cells. These clearly were but two
Vital details—though nobody cared much for
The future by that time, except us three.

You, Andrée Meraviglia, not quite three,
Left Heidelberg. Year, 1936.
That same decade you, Lo Ping, came to the fore
In the Spiritual Olympics, which you won.
My old black self I crave indulgence to
Withhold from limelight, acting on a belief I've

Lived by no less, no more, than by my five
Senses. Enough that circus music (BOOM-two-three)
Coursed through my veins. I saw how Timbuctoo
Would suffer an undue rainfall, 2.6
Inches. How in all of Fairbanks, wonder
of wonders, no polkas would be danced, or for

That matter no waltzes or rumbas, although four
Librarians, each on her first French 75,
Would do a maxixe (and a snappy one).
How, when on Lucca's greenest ramparts, three-
fold emotion prompting Renzo to choose from six
Older girls the blondest, call her *tu*,

It would be these blind eyes hers looked into
Widening in brief astonishment before
Love drugged her nerves with blossoms drawn from
    classics
Of Arab draftsmanship—small, ink-red, five-
Petaled blossoms blooming in clusters of three.
How she would want to show them to someone!

But one by one they're fading. I am too.
These three times thirteen lines I'll write down for
Fun, some May morning between five and six.

X. J. KENNEDY | b. 1929

Japanese Beetles

1 *Overheard in the Louvre*
Said the Victory of Samothrace,
What winning's worth this loss of face?

2 *Apocrypha*
Great Yahweh fingered through His Bible,
Thought on it. And filed suit for libel.

3 *To Someone Who Insisted I Look Up Someone*
I rang them up while touring Timbuctoo,
Those bosom chums to whom you're known as *Who*?

4 *Sex Manual*
By the cold glow that lit my lover's eye
I could read what page eight had said to try.

5
Time is that dentist fond of sweet desserts
Who, drill in hand, says, "Stop me if this hurts."

6 *At Colonus*
Stranger: That was a sacred altar!
        You dare plant buttocks there?
Oedipus: Where gods no more set table
        May man not make his chair?

7   *To a Now-Type Poet*
Your stoned head's least whim jotted down white-hot?
Enough confusion of my own I've got.

8   *Translator*
They say he knows, who renders Old High Dutch,
His own tongue only and of it not much.

9   *Parody: Herrick*
When Vestalina's thin white hand cuts cheese
The very mice go down upon their knees.

10   *To a Young Poet*
On solemn asses fall plush sinecures,
So keep a straight face and sit tight on yours.

11   *To an Angry God*
Lend me cruel light
That, tooling over syllables I write,
I do not skim forgivingly. Not spare,
But smite.

12   *A Late Call for Armaments*
As concertgoers at soft woodwinds cough,
In time of peace, militarists sound off.

13   *Aphasia*
  for C. F.
It gains on me like fat or growing bald,
This ailment of forgetting—what's it called?

14 *To a Hard Core Porn-Film Leading Man*
Obscure stone face, crowds cast you not a glance.
Disclose yourself—they'll know you! Drop your pants!

15 *Literary Cocktail Party*
Abuse pours in on all who leave the room,
Ill nature so abhors a vacuum.

16 *An Editor*
What do you call the taste of Peter Pitter?
A plastic spoon for straining Kitty Litter,
Whose even perforations let slip through
Never a hunk of stinking offal, true—
Just an innocuous wet-on residue.

17 *On a Given Book*
I slumbered with your sonnets on my bosom:
The net result of trying to peruse 'em.

18 *A Note on Contributors*
Writers of high renown, in *Playboy*'s hire,
    Who'd waylay men intent on spilling seed,
Remind us of Miss Prothero at the fire
    Offering the firemen something nice to read.

19 *Acumen*
What critic can be more acute
    Than T. P. Random-Carper
Who pokes his pencils up his chute
    And bumps-and-grinds 'em sharper?

20 *An Autobiographer*
With flattering mirror, while Medusa slakes
Her thirst for love, she petrifies her snakes.

21 *Sappho to a Mummy Wrapped in Papyrus*
Dull Pharaoh, rot in pride. Each stately line
Of your strict form lies packed in one of mine.
By priests regaled, by scarabs ravaged, sleep
Till time decide whose leftovers will keep.

22 *Conformity*
  after Baudelaire
The Belgians won't just copy. If
  Drink is in style they'll drink to drench
Their drawers, and when they catch a syph
  They'll double-dose, to be twice French.

23 *Two Lovers Proceed to Love Despite Their Sunburns*
With motion slow and gingerly they place
Their outward forms, broiled bright as carapace,
Like linesmen handling bared high-tension wires
Dreading the surges of abrupt desires.

24
None but the Spirit, moving and igniting,
Deserves the credit in creative writing.

Said

J. Alfred Prufrock to
Hugh Selwyn Mauberly,
'What ever happened to
Senlin, ought-nine?'

'One with the passion for
Orientalia?'
'Rather.' 'Losttrackofhim.'
'Pity.' 'Design.'

Said

Agatha Christie to
E. Phillips Oppenheim,
'Who is this Hemingway,
Who is this Proust?

Who is this Vladimir
Whatchamacallum, this
Neopostrealist
Rabble?' she groused.

Said

Dame Edith Evans to
Margaret Rutherford,
'Seance? Oh really, my
Dear, if there be

Nonhypothetical
Extraterrestrial
Parapsychologists,
They can call *me*.'

Said

J. Edgar Hoover to
Constable Dogberry,
'We are the *Law*. When they
Call us a pig,

We must impugn them for
Creditability.
After them! After them!
Jiggety-jig!'

High Renaissance

"Nomine Domini
Theotocopoulos,
None of these prelates can
Manage your name.

Change it. Appeal to their
Hellenophilia.
Sign it 'El Greco.' I'll
Slap on a frame."

Working Habits

Federico García Lorca
used to uncork a
bottle or two of wine
whenever the duende dwindled for a line.

James Joyce
would have preferred a choice
of brandies in decanters made by Tiffany's,
but rotgut was the shortcut to epiphanies.

The Later Henry James
bet shots of rum against himself in games
of how much can we pyramid upon a
given donné.

Little Dylan Thomas
didn't keep his promise
to stay out of Milk Wood.
He tried to drown the fact as best he could.

Anna Akhmatova
eyed the last shot of a
pre-war *cognac de champagne*.
'So much for you, little brandy. *Do svidanya*.'

T. S. Eliot
used to belly it
up to the nearest bar,
then make for a correlative objective in his car.

Proust
used
to
too.

Boston

Mr. Paul Verlaine?
We've come to fix your clerihew again.
No no no no, moi je m'appelle Verlaine.
Sure buddy, and I'm Richard Henry Dana.

On the Antiquity of Warfare

(For my son John, while he is thinking about the ROTC)

The celebrated Missing Link
made mincemeat of a few of us
I think. Therefore I am, I think
congenitally, cagey. *Sink
or swim! Troy gate or Tartarus!*
The Celebrated Missing link
arms. *Are you with us, boys?* And wink.
Is not the night sky glorious?

I think therefore I am. I think
I like it that way. Rinky-dink
escadrilles, shine on. Make a fuss.
The celebrated missing Link
Trainer patrol that hit the drink
south of El Paso lives. And thus
cogito ergo sum I think
lives, where they lined up in the clink
to forge the bright, the clangorous,
the celebrated missing link
"I Think Therefore I Am I Think"

one more time:

I think therefore I am I think
The celebrated Missing Link.
My socks don't match, my shit don't stink,
My landing brakes are on the blink,
But I could fly to Hell through ink

In a coal-fired kitchen sink.
So buck up, Tooey you dumb gink.
When the great game-plan hits a kink
And I am needed at the brink
I'll be there, feisty as a mink
With Memphis Rose and Lil the Chink
At Mama Juana's Roller Rink

      one more time.

I will stand tall. I will not shrink.
I'll sing until my scalp turns pink:
Rink a dink dink, rink a dink dink,
Last man in is a raaaaat fink.

And then if you don't mind I'll slink
Out a back door and hop a bus.
I'll hump and brawl and steal and cuss
And by the year two-thousand-plus
I'll be the most obstreperous
Old AWOL since Odysseus.

SOURCES AND ACKNOWLEDGMENTS

NOTES

INDEX

SOURCES AND ACKNOWLEDGMENTS

The following list identifies the source for each of the poems included in this volume and provides copyright information and acknowledgments. Great care has been taken to trace all owners of copyright material included in this book. If any have been inadvertently omitted or overlooked, acknowledgment will gladly be made in future printings.

Ambrose Bierce, *from* The Devil's Dictionary: *The Cynic's Word Book* (New York: Doubleday and Co., 1906).

Edwin Arlington Robinson, Two Men: *The Children of the Night* (New York: Charles Scribner's Sons, 1919). This book was first published in 1896. A Mighty Runner: *Captain Craig: Revised Edition with Additional Poems* (New York: The Macmillan Company, 1915). The collection first appeared in 1902. Miniver Cheevy: *The Town Down the River* (New York: Charles Scribner's Sons, 1910).

Carolyn Wells, Famous Baths and Bathers: *The New Yorker*, January 19, 1929.

Arthur Guiterman, Elegy; *from* The Lyric Baedeker: *The Mirthful Lyre* (New York: Harper and Brothers, 1918). Everything In Its Place: *The Oxford Book of American Light Verse*, edited by William Harmon (New York: Oxford University Press, 1979). On the Vanity of Earthly Greatness: *Gaily the Troubadour* (New York: E. P. Dutton and Co., 1936).

"Everything In Its Place" and "On the Vanity of Earthly Greatness" are copyright © Arthur Guiterman, reprinted with the permission of Richard E. Sclove.

Guy Wetmore Carryl, The Embarrassing Episode of Little Miss Muffet; The Harmonious Heedlessness of Little Boy Blue: *Mother Goose for Grown-Ups* (New York: Harper and Brothers, 1900).

Robert Frost, The Wrights' Biplane; In Divés' Dive; In a Poem: *Complete Poems of Robert Frost 1949* (New York: Henry Holt and Co., 1949). Copyright © 1949 by Henry Holt and Company. Reprinted with permission.

Don Marquis, the song of mehitabel; archy at the zoo; *from* mehitabel's extensive past: *archy & mehitabel* (Garden City, NY: Doubleday, Page and Co., 1927). Copyright © 1927 by Doubleday, a division of Random House, Inc. Used by permission of Doubleday, a division of Random House, Inc. ballade of the under side: *archy's life of mehitabel* (Garden City, NY: Doubleday, Doran and Co., 1933). Copyright © 1927, 1933 by Doubleday, a division of Random House, Inc. Used by permission of Doubleday, a division of Random House, Inc.

Vachel Lindsay, Factory Windows Are Always Broken: *The Congo and Other Poems* (New York: The Macmillan Company, 1914). A Colloquial Reply: To Any Newsboy; Niagara: *The Chinese Nightingale and Other Poems* (New York: The Macmillan Company, 1917). Kalamazoo: *Collected Poems*, revised and illustrated edition (New York: The Macmillan Co., 1925). "Kalamazoo" is copyright © 1925 the Estate of Vachel Lindsay and used by permission of Nicholas C. Lindsay, executor.

Franklin P. Adams, Us Potes: *In Other Words* (Garden City, NY: Doubleday, Page and Co., 1912). Ballade of Schopenhauer's Philosophy: *Weights and Measures* (Garden City, NY: Doubleday, Page and Co., 1917). The Rich Man: *Modern American Poetry*, edited by Louis Untermeyer (New York: Harcourt, Brace and Howe, 1919). "Lines Where Beauty Lingers"; To a Thesaurus: *The Melancholy Lute: Selected Songs of Thirty Years* (New York: The Viking Press, 1936). The last two poems are copyright © 1936 Anthony R. Adams and are used with permission.

Ezra Pound, An Immorality: *Ripostes* (London: Stephen Swift and Co., 1912). Ancient Music: *Lustra* (New York: Alfred A. Knopf, 1917).

T. S. Eliot, The Naming of Cats; Macavity: The Mystery Cat: *Old Possum's Book of Practical Cats* (London: Faber and Faber, 1939). Copyright © 1939 by T. S. Eliot, renewed 1967 by Esme Valerie Eliot, reprinted by permission of Harcourt, Inc.

Newman Levy, Tannhauser; Carmen; Rigoletto; Pelleas and Melisande: *Opera Guyed* (New York: Alfred A. Knopf, 1923). Copyright © 1923 by Alfred A. Knopf, Inc. and renewed 1951 by Newman Levy. Used by permission of Alfred A. Knopf, a division of Random House, Inc.

John Crowe Ransom, Survey of Literature: *Two Gentlemen in Bonds* (New York: Alfred A. Knopf, 1927). Also appears in *Selected Poems, Third Edition, Revised and Enlarged* by John Crowe Ransom, copyright © 1924, 1927 by Alfred A. Knopf, Inc. and renewed 1952, 1955 by John Crowe Ransom. Used by permission of Alfred A. Knopf, a division of Random House, Inc.

Samuel Hoffenstein, *from* Love Songs, at Once Tender and Informative; *from* The Notebook of a Schnook; *from* Poems in Praise of Practically Nothing; *from* Songs About Life and Brighter Things Yet; *from* Couplets, Rare, Medium, and Well-Done: *The Complete Poetry of Samuel Hoffenstein* (New York: Modern Library, 1954). The excerpts from "Love Songs, at Once Tender and Informative," "Poems in Praise of Practically Nothing," and "Songs About Life and Brighter Things Yet" were also published in *Poems in Praise of Practically Nothing*, copyright © 1928 by Samuel Hoffenstein, and are used by permission of Liveright Publishing Corporation. "The Sexes" from "Couplets, Rare, Medium, and Well-Done" was also published in *Year In, You're Out*, copyright © 1930 by Samuel Hoffenstein, and is used by permission of Liveright Publishing Corporation.

Christopher Morley, Elegy Written in a Country Coal-Bin: *Chimneysmoke* (New York: George H. Doran, 1921). "A Pre-Raphaelite": *What Cheer*, edited by David McCord (New York: Coward McCann, 1945). Reprinted by permission.

Maxwell Bodenheim, Upper Family: *Selected Poems of Maxwell Bodenheim 1914–1944* (New York: The Beechhurst Press, 1946).

Edna St. Vincent Millay, First Fig; Second Fig; Thursday; Grown-Up: *A Few Figs from Thistles* (New York: Harper and Brothers, 1922).

Morris Bishop, Ozymandias Revisited; We Have Been Here Before; "A joker who haunts Monticello"; Flowers of Rhetoric; Ah, To Be In . . .: *The Best of Bishop*, edited by Charlotte Putnam Reppert (Ithaca, NY: Cornell University Press, 1980). Eschatology: *What Cheer*, edited by David McCord (New York: Coward McCann, 1945).

Dorothy Parker, Portrait of the Artist; Chant for Dark Hours; Unfortunate Coincidence; Comment; Words of Comfort to be Scratched on a Mirror; News Item; Song of One of the Girls; Fighting Words; Inscription for the Ceiling of a Bedroom; Experience; Neither Bloody Nor Bowed; Bohemia; Story; Frustration; Résumé; One Perfect Rose; Ballade at Thirty-Five; Healed; Pour Prendre Congé; Coda; The Danger of Writing Defiant Verse; The Actress: *Complete Poems*, edited by Colleen Breese (New York: Penguin, 1999). Copyright © 1999 by The National Association for the Advancement of Colored People. Used by permission of Penguin, a division of Penguin Group (USA), Inc.

E. E. Cummings, "the way to hump a cow is not": *Complete Poems 1904–1962*, edited by George J. Firmage (New York: Liveright, 1991). Copyright 1940, © 1968, 1991 by the Trustees for the E. E. Cummings Trust. The poem quoted in the introduction, "mr u will not be missed," copyright 1944, © 1972, 1991 by the Trustess for the E. E. Cummings Trust. Both poems are taken from *Complete Poems: 1904–1962* by E. E. Cummings, edited by George J. Firmage. Used by permission of Liveright Publishing Corporation.

F. Scott Fitzgerald, Obit on Parnassus: *F. Scott Fitzgerald in His Own Time*, edited by Matthew J. Bruccoli and Jackson R. Bryer (Kent, OH: Kent State University Press, 1971). This poem was first published in *The New Yorker*, June 5, 1937. Copyright 1937 by F-R Pub. Corp. Copyright © renewed 1964 by Frances Scott Fitzgerald Lanahan. Reprinted by permission of Harold Ober Associates Incorporated.

David McCord, Sportif: *The New Yorker*, October 9, 1937. History of Education; Convalescence: *What Cheer* (New York: Coward McCann, 1945). Copyright © The Trustees of the Public Library of the City of Boston. All poems reprinted with permission.

John Wheelwright, Week End Bid I; Week End Bid II; Lion: *Collected Poems*, edited by Alvin H. Rosenfeld (New York: New Directions, 1972). Copyright © 1971 by Louise Wheelwright Damon. Reprinted by permission of New Directions Publishing Corp.

E. B. White, Marble-Top: *The Lady Is Cold* (New York: Harper and Brothers, 1929). I Paint What I See; Village Revisited: *Poems and Sketches of E. B. White* (New York: Harper and Row, 1981). All poems reprinted by permission of International Creative Management, Inc. Copyright © 1929, 1981. Reprinted by permission of the E. B. White Estate.

Kenneth Fearing, Old Story; Death and Transfiguration of Fourteenth Street: *Complete Poems*, edited by Robert M. Ryley (Orono, ME: National Poetry Foundation, 1994). Aphrodite Metropolis (III); Ballad of the Salvation Army; Cultural Notes: *Angel Arms* (New York: Coward McCann, 1929). Dirge: *Poems* (New York: Dynamo, 1935). Copyright © 1994 by Jubal Fearing and Phoebe Fearing. All poems reprinted by permission of the National Poetry Foundation.

Ogden Nash, Spring Comes to Murray Hill (© 1930): *Hard Lines* (New York: Simon and Schuster, 1931). Watchman, What of the First First Lady (© 1931): *Free Wheeling* (New York: Simon and Schuster, 1931). A Necessary Dirge (© 1935): *The Primrose Path* (New York: Simon and Schuster, 1935). No Wonder Our Fathers Died (© 1936); The Song of Songs (© 1935): *I'm a Stranger Here Myself* (Boston: Little, Brown and Co., 1938). Please Pass the Biscuit (© 1942); The Termite (© 1942); A

The following is a list of typographical errors in the source texts that have been corrected, cited by page and line number: 45.4, laughter.; 46.16, ukelele; 46.27, saxaphone; 49.25, Say's; 55.5, Pellas; 169.6, Eyed; 169.7, Pre-war.

NOTES

1.9–10   The cur foretells . . . the lea]   Cf. Thomas Gray, "Elegy in a Country Churchyard," lines 1-2: "The curfew tolls the knell of parting day, / The lowing herd winds slowly o'er the lea."

2.7   Melchizedek]   King of Salem who blessed Abraham in Genesis 14:18–20.

2.11   Ucalegon]   A Trojan in Virgil's *Aeneid*, Book II.

3.2   *Nicarchus*]   Greek epigrammatist of the 1st century C.E.

5.21   Ettrick shephe'd]   James Hogg (1770–1835), Scottish poet and novelist known as "the Ettrick Shepherd."

14.1   "The Maiden's Prayer;"]   Popular piano piece by the Polish composer Tekla Bandarzewska (1838–61).

14.3   "Die Wacht am Rhein"]   "Watch on the Rhine," patriotic German song; words by Max Schneckenburger (1819–49) and music by Karl Wilhelm (1815–73).

16.7   Divés]   Latin for "rich," and the name popularly given to the unnamed rich man in the parable of Lazarus (cf. Luke 16:19–31).

31.28   Lorna Doone, Rosy O'Grady]   Lorna Doone, eponymous heroine of R. D. Blackmore's 1869 novel; Rosy O'Grady, subject of the popular song "Sweet Rosie O'Grady" (1896), with words and music by Maud Nugent.

31.29   Orphant Annie]   The subject of James Whitcomb Riley's poem "Little Orphant Annie."

33.2   Potes]   Poets. Adams' title may play on the Latin *ut potes*, "as you are able."

34.20   The Conning Tower] Adams' column in the New York *Herald Tribune* and several other newspapers, which ran from 1913 until 1938.

37.8–38.12   Tell me not . . . phantom of delight] The lines are from Richard Lovelace, "To Lucasta, Going to the Wars"; Edmund Waller, "On a Girdle"; the anonymous lyric "Get Up and Bar the Door"; Kate Putnam Osgood, "Driving Home the Cows"; Rudyard Kipling, "The Vampire"; Edwin Arlington Robinson, "The Master"; George Etherege, "To a Lady, Asking Him How Long He Would Love Her"; William Wordsworth, "To a Butterfly"; Robert Burns; Samuel Daniel; Lascelles Abercombie, "Song from 'Judith'"; Oliver Wendell Holmes, "Old Ironsides"; Allen Ramsay, "Song"; Thomas Hood, "Ruth"; William Wordsworth; Thomas Hood; Robert Louis Stevenson; Alexander Pope, "Epigram Engraved on the Collar of a Dog Which I Gave to His Royal Highness"; Ralph Waldo Emerson, "Concord Hymn"; Ralph Waldo Emerson, epigraph to "Friendship"; John Hookham Frere, "The Boy and the Wolf"; Walter Scott, "Marmion"; Robert Browning, "Memorabilia"; Thomas Carew, "Song"; Thomas Lodge, "Rosalind's Madrigal"; Charles Sedley, "Song"; George Darley, "Last Night"; William Wordsworth.

39.12   icummen in] Cf. the medieval English round that begins: "Sumer is icumen in / Lhude sing cuccu." Pound's poem parodies the rest of the text as well.

44.24   The Napoleon of Crime] Cf. Sherlock Holmes' remark to Dr. Watson concerning the archcriminal Professor Moriarty in Arthur Conan Doyle's "The Final Problem": "He is the Napoleon of crime, Watson."

58.5   Maid of Gotham] Cf. Lord Byron's lyric: "Maid of Athens, ere we part, / Give, oh give me back my heart."

59.8   D.G.] *Deo Gratias*: Thank God.

64.18   Book of Knowledge] Encyclopedia for children, first published by the Grolier Society in 1911.

65.23   bunghole] Cf. *Hamlet* V.i.203-4: "the noble ghost of Alexander . . . stopping a bunghole."

68.2   Elegy Written] See note 1.9–10.

69.4   Elizabeth Siddal] Artist (1829–62) who was the model and, briefly, the wife of Dante Gabriel Rossetti.

75.14   We Have Been Here Before] Cf. Dante Gabriel Rossetti's "Sudden Light," line 1: "I have been here before."

77.22–23   Where . . . vile] Cf. "Missionary Hymn" ("From Greenland's icy mountains") by Reginald Heber (1783–1826): "Though every prospect pleases, / And only man is vile."

81.12   Marie of Roumania] Granddaughter of Queen Victoria (1875–1938) who married the king of Romania and later published her memoirs.

81.16   Ninon] The French courtesan and salon hostess Ninon de Lenclos (1620–1705).

82.8   Kitty O'Shea] Katherine Page O'Shea, wife of Captain William O'Shea, an advocate of Irish home rule; he divorced her in 1890 for her affair with Irish leader Charles Parnell.

82.9   poor Nell] Eleanor (Nell) Gwynn (1650–87), actress and mistress of Charles II.

89.1   Pour Prendre Congé] Taking leave to depart.

89.4   Dolores] "Our Lady of Pain," the addressee of Swinburne's poem of the same name.

98.25   Realms of Gold] Cf. John Keats, "On First Looking into Chapman's Homer," line 1: "Much have I traveled in the Realms of Gold."

100.9   *William Lyon Phelps*] Phelps (1865–1943) was a Yale English professor whose popular guides to literature included *What I Like in Poetry* (1934).

100.21 Miss Lulu Betts] Novel (1920) by Zona Gale (1874–1938).

100.22 *Witching Hour*] *The Witching Hour*, novel (1907) by Augustus Thomas (1857–1934).

100.23 Second Volume] A. E. Housman's *Last Poems* (1922).

100.25 *Bob, Son of Battle*] American title of *Owd Bob*, an 1898 novel about an English collie by Alfred Ollivant (1874–1927).

101.1   *Jar of Dreams*] Book of verse published in 1923.

101.2   *Waves of Unrest*] *Songs of Unrest*, book of verse published in 1923.

107.3–4 Charlotte Endymion Porter . . . Helen Archibald Clark] Co-editors of editions of Shakespeare and Browning; Porter was also co-founder in 1889 of *Poet Lore*, a magazine primarily devoted to British writers.

101.5   Anna Hempstead Branch] American poet (1875–1937); see her poem "In the Beginning Was the Word": "It took me ten days / To read the Bible through."

102.16–17 *Removal . . . Year 1933*] Nelson Rockefeller commissioned Mexican artist Diego Rivera to paint a mural in the lobby of the RCA Building in the spring of 1933. When Rivera included a portrait of Lenin in the work, Rockefeller asked him to remove it. After Rivera refused, work on the mural was stopped and it was covered in canvas. In February 1934 the management of Rockefeller Center had the mural broken up and discarded.

103.14 Mordaunt Hall] Film and drama critic for *The New York Times* during the 1920s and 30s.

109.24 Max Nordau] Nordau (1849–1923) was the author of *Degeneration* (1895), an attack on modern art.

111.4   Carbide]   Shares in the Union Carbon and Carbide Company.

119.21–22   When Duty whispers low, Thou must]   Cf. Ralph Waldo Emerson, "Voluntaries": "When Duty whispers low, *Thou must*, / The youth replies, *I can*."

122.24   Lalage]   A young woman praised by the Roman poet Horace in his Book of Odes I, 22.

127.5   Townsends and Coughlins and Longs]   Francis Townsend (1867–1960) advanced a proposal in 1934 for a national pension plan that won widespread support. Father Charles Coughlin (1891–1979), a popular radio speaker, founded the National Union for Social Justice in 1934. Senator Huey Long (1893–1935) introduced his "Share Our Wealth" plan for radical income redistribution in 1934.

128.3   When . . . spent]   The opening line of Milton's Sonnet 19, on his blindness.

130.11   "*Sweet Adeline*"]   Song (1903) by Harry Armstrong and Richard H. Gerard.

131.21   "Danny Deever"]   Poem by Rudyard Kipling.

136.18   McDow'll]   The MacDowell Colony for writers, composers, and artists in Peterborough, New Hampshire.

136.25   Mansfield]   Mt. Mansfield, in the Green Mountains of Vermont.

140.2   Helen . . . to me]   Opening line of Edgar Allan Poe's "To Helen."

144.26   Middle Earth]   In Germanic mythology, the natural world inhabited by humans.

145.6   As stout as Cortez]   Cf. John Keats, "On First Looking into Chapman's Homer": "Or like stout Cortez."

146.17   *Mens sana*]   "A sound mind," the first part of the Latin phrase that concludes *in corpore sano*, "in a sound body."

146.18   *Qui mal y pense*]   "Who thinks evil," from *Honi soit qui mal y pense*, "Shame to him who thinks evil," the motto of the Order of the Garter.

150.15   Bosie]   Wilde's lover Lord Alfred Douglas (1870–1945).

154.12   Mme. de Maintenon]   Françoise d'Aubigné, marquise de Maintenon (1635–1719) secretly married Louis XIV in 1683 and later founded a school for girls at Saint-Cyr.

155.12   Gustav von Aschenbach]   Composer who is the protagonist of Thomas Mann's novella *Death in Venice*.

157.2–3   Theme by William Carlos Williams]   Cf. Williams' "This Is Just To Say."

158.10–11   "Est-ce . . . la joie?"]   "Don't you want delight?"

164.19–20   Miss Prothero . . . nice to read]   In "A Child's Christmas in Wales" by Dylan Thomas.

166.3–4   J. Alfred Prufrock to Hugh Selwyn Mauberly]   The subject of "The Love Song of J. Alfred Prufrock" by T. S. Eliot; fictional minor English poet, the subject of a sequence of poems by Ezra Pound.

166.6   Senlin]   The subject of the poem "Senlin: A Biography" by Conrad Aiken.

167.2–3   Edith Evans to Margaret Rutherford]   Evans (1888–1976) and Rutherford (1892–1972) were British stage and screen actresses.

169.8   *Do svidanya*]   "Goodbye."

INDEX OF POETS, TITLES, AND FIRST LINES

ABOUT THIS SERIES

The American Poets Project offers, for the first time in our history, a compact national library of American poetry. Selected and introduced by distinguished poets and scholars, elegant in design and textually authoritative, the series makes widely available the full scope of our poetic heritage.

For other titles in the American Poets Project, or for information on subscribing to the series, please visit: www.americanpoetsproject.org.

ABOUT THE PUBLISHER

The Library of America, a nonprofit publisher, is dedicated to preserving America's best and most significant writing in handsome, enduring volumes, featuring authoritative texts. For a free catalog, to subscribe to the series, or to learn how you can help support The Library's mission, please visit www.loa.org or write: The Library of America, 14 East 60th Street, New York, NY 10022.

AMERICAN POETS PROJECT

EDNA ST. VINCENT MILLAY: SELECTED POEMS
J. D. McClatchy, editor
ISBN 1-931082-34-0

POETS OF WORLD WAR II
Harvey Shapiro, editor
ISBN 1-931082-34-0

KARL SHAPIRO: SELECTED POEMS
John Updike, editor
ISBN 1-931082-34-0

WALT WHITMAN: SELECTED POEMS
Harold Bloom, editor
ISBN 1-931082-32-4

EDGAR ALLAN POE: POEMS AND POETICS
Richard Wilbur, editor
ISBN 1-931082-51-0

YVOR WINTERS: SELECTED POEMS
Thom Gunn, editor
ISBN 1-931082-50-2

AMERICAN WITS: AN ANTHOLOGY OF LIGHT VERSE
John Hollander, editor
ISBN 1-931082-49-9